Canadian Human Rights in a Nutshell

with a copy of the Canadian Human Rights Act and the Canadian Charter of Rights and Freedoms

Bryan Law LLD

Fox College of Business

© Bryan Law, Fox College of Business

All rights reserved. No part of this book may be reproduced in any form by any means or used in any information storage and retrieval system without the written permission of the writer.

First edition: December 2020
Revised edition: November 2022

Fox College of Business

Disclaimer

Fox College of Business and Bryan Law are not engaged in rendering legal or other professional services, and this book should not be relied upon as providing such advice. We strongly urge that you seek professional advice prior to acting on the information contained herein.

The information contained herein has been obtained from sources which we believe are reliable, but we cannot guarantee its accuracy or completeness. Fox College of Business, Bryan Law and every person involved in the creation of this book disclaim any warranty as to the accuracy, completeness and currency of the contents of this book. We also disclaim all liability in respect of the results of any action taken or not taken in reliance upon information in this book.

The Department of Justice, Government of Canada, has the copyright to the texts of the relevant laws contained in this book. The reprint provisions in this book are copied or reproduced under permission granted by the Department of Justice. No such reproduction shall indicate that the Department of Justice is in any way responsible for the accuracy or reliability of the reproduction, nor shall any such reproduction indicate that it was made with the endorsement of, or in affiliation with, the Department of Justice.

Preface

I want to take this opportunity to thank my sister, Jessica Law, for giving me the photo of her painting, *Thinking*, to use as the image on the front cover of this book.

Jessica is a novel abstract expressionist artist who distinguishes herself in the modern water-ink community by painting vivid colours with extensive shades of ink. Combined with the unique composition skills that she utilizes in her paintings, her works touch the minds of those who see them and evoke feelings of awe, spirituality, and connection.

Thinking was created during the COVID-19 pandemic; it represents that our minds function in very different dimensions and will probably be more dynamic than ever.

To view more of Jessica's paintings, you can visit jessicafylaw.com

Painting on the Front Cover

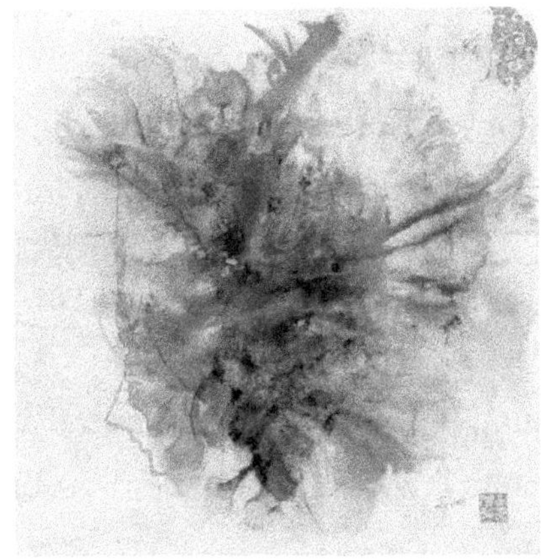

Artist:	Jessica Law
Title:	Thinking
Medium:	Mixed media on canvas
Size:	50 cm x 50 cm

Website: jessicafylaw.com

Painting on the Back Cover

Artist:	Bryan Law
Title:	3D Inuksuk
Medium:	100% Acrylic on canvas
Size:	8" x 10"

Website: transparentpaintings.com

Bryan K. Law BSc, LLM, LLD

Bryan is a well-known author, consultant and educator in Canada and has a diversified professional background.

Bryan is a management consultant with more than 20 years of experience. He is also a legal researcher in various areas, including contract law, environmental law, human rights law, labour law, privacy law and real estate law.

Different education institutions have hired Bryan to provide his business management, law and real estate expertise. Bryan has authored over 20 books in various disciplines, including the best-selling *Differential Cogitation, Guide to Employment Law in Hong Kong, Fatal Mistakes in Home Buying & Real Estate Investment, Why Do Some Franchises Fail, Feng Shui 123 and more.*

Bryan's wide-ranging knowledge and professional experience, coupled with humorous presentation skills, have also placed him in demand as a professional speaker.

Table of Contents

Chapter

1. Introduction 1

2. What Constitutes Human Rights Law 9

3. Age 23

4. Creed 35

5. Disability 47

6. Race and Related Grounds 57

7. Sex and Related Grounds 67

8. Other Grounds 75

9. Indigenous People 85

Appendix

I. Glossary of Human Rights Terms 95

II. Canadian Human Rights Act 107

III. Canadian Charter of Rights and Freedoms 169

1. Introduction

Starting from the genocide of Indigenous people[1] when colonizing North America, the discrimination and suppression of other ethnic groups by the Americans have shown no sign of stopping.[2] Incidents of racial discrimination in the United States can be said to be endless.[3] Because society discriminates against Blacks systematically and law enforcement agencies continue to have violence against Blacks, a social movement in protest against police brutality incidents and all racially motivated violence against Black people has spread to almost every Western country.[4]

Although a well-known statement on human rights was found in the second paragraph of the United States Declaration of

---

[1] "When Native Americans Were Slaughtered in the Name of 'Civilization'", A&E Television Networks, last updated August 16, 2019, https://www.history.com/news/native-americans-genocide-united-states

[2] "United States war crimes", Wikipedia, last accessed October 13, 2023, https://en.wikipedia.org/wiki/United_States_war_crimes

[3] "Discrimination in the United States", Wikipedia, last accessed October 13, 2023, https://en.wikipedia.org/wiki/Discrimination_in_the_United_States

[4] "Black Lives Matter", Wikipedia, last accessed October 13, 2023, https://en.wikipedia.org/wiki/Black_Lives_Matter

Independence[5] , which stated that "*all men are created equal*",[6] that concept established in 1776 did not apply to non-white people. Slavery was still allowed until Abraham Lincoln[7] abolished it in 1865. Today, human rights in the United States are still not protected well enough, which invites criticism.

For example, golf is one of the most popular single sports in the United States.[8] Although three out of the four major international golf championships[9] are held in the United States, the golf industry in the United States is full of sexism and racial discrimination.

Since its opening, the famous Shoal Creek Club[10] has never had a female member until 2009. It only accepted two female members in 2009, and they are the only two female members so

---

5 "United States Declaration of Independence", Wikipedia, last accessed October 13, 2023, https://en.wikipedia.org/wiki/United_States_Declaration_of_Independence

6 "All men are created equal", Wikipedia, last accessed October 13, 2023, https://en.wikipedia.org/wiki/All_men_are_created_equal

7 "Thirteenth Amendment to the United States Constitution", Wikipedia, last accessed October 13, 2023, https://en.wikipedia.org/wiki/Thirteenth_Amendment_to_the_United_States_Constitution

8 "Sports in the United States", Wikipedia, last accessed October 13, 2023, https://en.wikipedia.org/wiki/Sports_in_the_United_States

9 "Men's major golf championships", Wikipedia, last accessed October 13, 2023, https://en.wikipedia.org/wiki/Men%27s_major_golf_championships

10 "Shoal Creek Club", Wikipedia, last accessed October 13, 2023, https://en.wikipedia.org/wiki/Shoal_Creek_Club

far. Another equally famous Augusta Golf Club[11] also did not accept female members until 2012. Coincidentally, among the first two female members of the two golf clubs, one of them is the former Secretary of State Condoleezza Rice.[12] Another famous club, Cypress Points Club,[13] still does not accept Black people as members. Allowing such practices is allowing sexism and racial discrimination in disguise.

Historically, India's caste system[14] divided its people into four different classes,[15] namely Brahmin,[16] Kshatriya,[17] Vaishya,[18] and Shudra.[19] Brahmins specialized as priests and teachers and were at the head of the hierarchy. Kshatriyas were warriors and rulers. They ranked second in the caste system. Vaishyas were farmers, traders and merchants. They ranked third in the system.

---

11 "Augusta National Golf Club", Wikipedia, last accessed October 13, 2023, https://en.wikipedia.org/wiki/Augusta_National_Golf_Club

12 "Condoleezza Rice", Wikipedia, last accessed October 13, 2023, https://en.wikipedia.org/wiki/Condoleezza_Rice

13 "Cypress Point Club", Wikipedia, last accessed October 13, 2023, https://en.wikipedia.org/wiki/Cypress_Point_Club

14 "Caste system in India", Wikipedia, last accessed October 13, 2023, https://en.wikipedia.org/wiki/Caste_system_in_India

15 "What is India's caste system?", BBC, last updated June 19, 2019, https://www.bbc.com/news/world-asia-india-35650616

16 "Brahmin", Wikipedia, last accessed October 13, 2023, https://en.wikipedia.org/wiki/Brahmin

17 "Kshatriya", Wikipedia, last accessed October 13, 2023, https://en.wikipedia.org/wiki/Kshatriya

18 "Vaishya", Wikipedia, last accessed October 13, 2023, https://en.wikipedia.org/wiki/Vaishya

19 "Shudra", Wikipedia, last accessed October 13, 2023, https://en.wikipedia.org/wiki/Shudra

Sudras were peasants and labourers. They had the lowest status among the four.

Later, with the development of society, various castes branched into many levels. In addition to the four major castes, there is another type of people excluded from the castes called Dalit[20] or untouchable. They have the lowest social status and are most discriminated against by society. Most of them are street sweepers, latrine cleaners and coolies.

Although Article 15 of the Constitution of India stipulates that *The State shall not discriminate against any citizen on grounds only of religion, race, caste, sex, place of birth or any of them*[21], and Article 17 also states *"Untouchability" is abolished and its practice in any form is forbidden,*[22] discrimination based on the caste system is still a common problem in India.

The punishment of refusal to recognize the caste relationship may cause serious consequences, such as being publicly lynched to death by family members. Marriages between

---

[20] "Dalit", Wikipedia, last accessed October 13, 2023 https://en.wikipedia.org/wiki/Dalit

[21] "The Constitution of India", Government of India, last accessed October 13, 2023, https://www.india.gov.in/sites/upload_files/npi/files/coi_part_full.pdf

[22] Ditto

different castes may also lead to large-scale attacks on lower-caste communities.[23]

The caste is hereditary. For thousands of years, the caste system has profoundly impacted the daily lives and customs of billions of people. Racial discrimination has not been eliminated, especially in vast rural areas. Similar caste systems also exist in Nepal and Sri Lanka.[24]

Although The Constitution of France[25] states that *It shall ensure the equality of all citizens before the law, without distinction of origin, race or religion*, racism is still regarded by many as an important social issue in French society. Racism against Jews has a long history in France, and other targets include Algerians, Berbers and Arabs.[26]

Racism in France is also a hot issue. The French National Human Rights Commission reported in 2016 that 8% of French people believe that certain races are superior to others.[27] It is

---

[23] "Caste Discrimination: A Global Concern", Human Rights Watch for the United Nations, last accessed October 13, 2023, https://www.hrw.org/reports/2001/globalcaste/caste0801-03.htm

[24] Ditto

[25] "France's Constitution of 1958 with Amendments through 2008", Constitute, last accessed October 13, 2023, https://www.constituteproject.org/constitution/France_2008.pdf

[26] "Racism in France", Wikipedia, last accessed October 13, 2023, https://en.wikipedia.org/wiki/Racism_in_France

[27] Ditto

believed that the terrorist attacks in France in 2015[28] led to an increase in the number of people with Islamophobia,[29] and the strong social opposition to Muslims increased the number of racist acts. According to a survey conducted by the French National Human Rights Commission, 34% of the French population has a negative attitude toward Islam. Half of them believe that Islam is a menace to their national identity. Besides, 41% of the people believe that Jews have a singular relationship with money, while 20% of the population believe that Jews have too much power in France.

Like the United States, the United Kingdom has a history of enslaving Africans.[30] Although there is legislation such as the Human Rights Act 1998[31] and the Race Relations (Amendment) Act[32] to promote and protect racial equality, and UK Prime Minister Johnson said that the United Kingdom is not a racist country, many Black Britons disagree.[33] According to a 2014

---

[28] "November 2015 Paris attacks", Wikipedia, last accessed October 13, 2023, https://en.wikipedia.org/wiki/November_2015_Paris_attacks

[29] "Islamophobia", Wikipedia, last accessed October 13, 2023, https://en.wikipedia.org/wiki/Islamophobia

[30] "Slavery in Britain", Wikipedia, last accessed October 13, 2023, https://en.wikipedia.org/wiki/Slavery_in_Britain

[31] "Human Rights Act 1998", Government of the United Kingdom, last accessed October 13, 2023, https://www.legislation.gov.uk/ukpga/1998/42/contents

[32] "Race Relations (Amendment) Act 2000", Government of the United Kingdom, last accessed October 13, 2023, https://www.legislation.gov.uk/ukpga/2000/34/contents

[33] "Boris Johnson says the UK isn't a racist country. Black Britons disagree", The Independent, last updated June 9, 2020,

British Social Attitudes survey,[34] one-third of Britons admit to being racially prejudiced.[35]

Racial discrimination happens all over the world, including in communist countries. In Vietnam, the international society has accused the Vietnamese government of discriminating[36] against the Chams,[37] the Vietnamese Montagnard,[38] and the Khmer Krom.[39]

Because of the war crimes committed in the Second World War, the United Nations drafted the Universal Declaration of Human Rights (UDHR)[40] to set out the fundamental human rights to be universally protected. It was proclaimed in 1948, and all Member States of the United Nations pledged to work together to promote it. Today, it has been translated into over 500 languages. Since all the countries have different human rights issues, many

---

https://www.independent.co.uk/life-style/boris-johnson-racism-uk-george-floyd-protests-black-lives-matter-a9556756.html

34 "British Social Attitudes 36", NatCen Social Research, last accessed October 13, 2023, https://www.natcen.ac.uk/our-research/research/british-social-attitudes/

35 "One third of Britons 'admit being racially prejudiced'", BBC, last updated May 28, 2014, https://www.bbc.com/news/uk-27599401

36 "Racism in Vietnam", Wikipedia, last accessed October 13, 2023, https://en.wikipedia.org/wiki/Racism_in_Vietnam

37 "Chams", Wikipedia, last accessed October 13, 2023, https://en.wikipedia.org/wiki/Chams

38 "Montagnard (Vietnam)", Wikipedia, last accessed October 13, 2023, https://en.wikipedia.org/wiki/Montagnard_(Vietnam)

39 "Khmer Krom", Wikipedia, last accessed October 13, 2023, https://en.wikipedia.org/wiki/Khmer_Krom

40 "Universal Declaration of Human Rights", United Nations, last accessed October 13, 2023, https://www.un.org/en/universal-declaration-human-rights/

countries have started reviewing their human rights policies after the proclamation of UDHR, and Canada was one among them.

2. What Constitutes Human Rights Law

Human rights[41] refer to the rights that individuals or groups deserve because they are human beings. According to the United Nations,

> "*Human rights are rights inherent to all human beings, regardless of race, sex, nationality, ethnicity, language, religion, or any other status. Human rights include the right to life and liberty, freedom from slavery and torture, freedom of opinion and expression, the right to work and education, and many more. Everyone is entitled to these rights, without discrimination*".[42]

The Need for Human Rights Law

Many countries have passed legislation to protect human rights within their jurisdiction. Canada is one of the well-known countries that protect and promote human rights. However, like most countries, it took a long time for Canada to establish a well-protected human rights system.

---

[41] "Human rights", Wikipedia, last accessed October 13, 2023, https://en.wikipedia.org/wiki/Human_rights

[42] "Human rights", United Nations, last accessed October 13, 2023, https://www.un.org/en/sections/issues-depth/human-rights/

The British North America (BNA) Act,[43] passed by the British Parliament in 1867 to create the Dominion of Canada, did not address any issue of human rights. In 1928, the Supreme Court of Canada even ruled that women were not "persons" according to the BNA Act, so women in Canada were ineligible for appointment to the Senate. The Famous Five[44] appealed to the Judicial Committee of the Privy Council in Britain in 1929, and the British Privy Council decided that women were, in fact, "persons" under the Act.[45]

The Unemployment Relief Act, passed by the British Columbia government in 1931 to distribute relief during the Great Depression,[46] contained the first anti-discrimination provision in Canadian law. Section 8 of the act stated that "*in no case shall discrimination be made in the employment of any persons by reason of their political affiliation*".[47] In 1932, the act was amended to expand the prohibition on race and religion. Section 10

---

[43] "Constitution Act, 1867", The Canadian Encyclopedia, last updated April 24, 2020, https://thecanadianencyclopedia.ca/en/article/constitution-act-1867

[44] "Famous Five", The Canadian Encyclopedia, last updated June 4, 2015, https://www.thecanadianencyclopedia.ca/en/article/famous-5

[45] "Persons Case", The Canadian Encyclopedia, last updated October 18, 2019, https://www.thecanadianencyclopedia.ca/en/article/persons-case

[46] "Human Rights Law", University of Alberta, last accessed November 4, 2020, https://historyofrights.ca/history/human-rights-law/2/

[47] "British Columbia Unemployment Relief Act 1931", University of Alberta, last accessed November 4, 2020, https://historyofrights.ca/wp-content/uploads/statutes/BC_Unemploy1.pdf

of the act stated, "*In no case shall discrimination be made or permitted in the employment of any persons by reason of their political affiliation, race, or religious views*".[48] Although this act prohibited racial and religious discrimination, it was limited to employment and was only a provincial law.

The lack of human rights laws in Canada was exposed in *Christie v. The York Corporation*[49] in 1939. The claimant was refused service in a tavern because he was Black. The tavern staff refused him for the sole reason that they had been instructed not to serve "coloured persons". The claimant took the case to court and claimed the sum of $200 for the humiliation he suffered. The trial judge awarded him $25 damages, and the tavern appealed. The Court of Appeal held that, as a general rule, in the absence of any specific law, a merchant or trader was free to carry on his business in the manner he conceived to be best for that business. Therefore, the Court of Appeal reversed the original judgment. The claimant appealed to the Supreme Court of Canada, but his case was dismissed as there was no law to protect the claimant's rights at that time.

---

[48] "British Columbia Unemployment Relief Act 1932", University of Alberta, last accessed November 4, 2020, https://historyofrights.ca/wp-content/uploads/statutes/BC_Unemploy2.pdf

[49] 1939 CanLII 39 (SCC), [1940] SCR 139

The Brief Timeline

The first law solely dedicated to anti-discrimination in Canada was passed in Ontario in 1944.[50] The Racial Discrimination Act prohibited the display of discriminatory signs and advertisements. Although the whole act had only two pages,[51] it was a breakthrough and milestone in protecting human rights in Canada.

In 1947, Saskatchewan passed the Saskatchewan Bill of Rights[52] to protect fundamental rights and freedoms and prohibit various discriminations on the grounds of race, creed, religion, colour, or ethnic or national origin. Manitoba, Nova Scotia, British Columbia, New Brunswick, Quebec, North-West Territories and Alberta also passed anti-discrimination-related legislation in the next two decades. However, most of those laws were just related to employment.

---

[50] "The Evolution of Human Rights in Canada", Canadian Human Rights Commission, last accessed November 4, 2020, https://www.chrc-ccdp.gc.ca/eng/content/evolution-human-rights-canada

[51] "Racial Discrimination Act", University of Alberta, last accessed November 4, 2020, https://historyofrights.ca/wp-content/uploads/statutes/ON_Racial.pdf

[52] "Saskatchewan Bill of Rights", Wikipedia, last accessed October 13, 2023, https://en.wikipedia.org/wiki/Saskatchewan_Bill_of_Rights

The Canadian Human Rights Act[53] was passed in 1977 to ensure equal opportunity for individuals who may be discriminated against by other people based on a set of prohibited grounds. With the Canadian Charter of Rights and Freedoms[54] passed in 1982, forming the first part of the Constitution Act 1982,[55] Canada became one of the countries in the world that best protects the human rights of its citizens. Below is the brief timeline of anti-discrimination legislation in Canada up to the Canadian Charter of Rights and Freedoms was passed.

1931 Unemployment Relief Act (British Columbia)
1944 Ontario Racial Discrimination Act
1947 Saskatchewan Bill of Rights
1951 Ontario Fair Employment Practices Act
1953 Canada Fair Employment Practices Act
1953 Manitoba Fair Employment Practices Act
1954 Ontario Fair Accommodation Practices Act
1955 Nova Scotia Fair Employment Practices Act
1956 British Columbia Fair Employment Practices Act
1956 New Brunswick Fair Employment Practices Act
1956 Saskatchewan Fair Accommodation Practices Act

---

53 "Canadian Human Rights Act", Wikipedia, last accessed October 13, 2023, https://en.wikipedia.org/wiki/Canadian_Human_Rights_Act

54 "Canadian Charter of Rights and Freedoms", Wikipedia, last accessed October 13, 2023, https://en.wikipedia.org/wiki/Canadian_Charter_of_Rights_and_Freedoms

55 "Constitution of Canada", Wikipedia, last accessed October 13, 2023, https://en.wikipedia.org/wiki/Constitution_of_Canada

1959 Nova Scotia Fair Accommodation Practices Act
1959 New Brunswick Fair Accommodation Practices Act
1960 Manitoba Fair Accommodation Practices Act
1960 Canadian Bill of Rights
1961 British Columbia Public Accommodation Practices Act
1962 Human Rights Code (Ontario)
1964 Quebec Act Respecting Discrimination in Employment
1966 North-West Territories Fair Practices Ordinance
1966 Alberta Human Rights Act
1973 Human Rights Act (British Columbia)
1976 Quebec Charter of Human Rights and Freedoms
1977 Canadian Human Rights Act
1982 Canadian Charter of Rights and Freedoms

Relevant Legislation

There are two levels of jurisdictions in Canada to deal with human rights legislation: the federal and the provincial or territorial governments. Federal laws apply to the whole country; provincial and territorial laws are local and only apply to that province or territory. While the Canadian Human Rights Act[56] and the Canadian Charter of Rights and Freedom[57] are federal laws and

[56] "Canadian Human Rights Act (R.S.C., 1985, c. H-6)", Government of Canada, last updated October 29, 2020, https://laws-lois.justice.gc.ca/eng/acts/h-6/

[57] "Constitution Acts, 1867 to 1982", Government of Canada, last updated October 29, 2020, https://laws-lois.justice.gc.ca/eng/const/page-15.html

apply to all jurisdictions in Canada, some provinces still maintain their own human rights law. However, a case heard in a province or territory may still consider the Code and case laws of other provinces and territories.

The Canadian Human Rights Act and the Canadian Charter of Rights and Freedoms set the basic framework of human rights protection that applies to every province and territory. Each province and territory may have its own law and code to detail human rights protection further within its jurisdiction. In other words, if a province or territory has its own set of human rights laws, the people in that province or territory will have two sets of rules to follow. One is federal law, which gives the foundation. Another one is the provincial or territorial law to cover more aspects. For example, the Government of Ontario passed its own Human Rights Code[58] and other relevant laws, such as the Accessibility for Ontarians with Disabilities Act,[59] to provide better protection for disabled people.

There are different legislation at the federal, provincial, and territorial levels to deal with protections or discriminations related to human rights. The following are some of the major acts related to human rights in different jurisdictions:

---

[58] "Human Rights Code, R.S.O. 1990, c. H.19", Government of Ontario, last accessed October 13, 2023, https://www.ontario.ca/laws/statute/90h19

[59] "Accessibility for Ontarians with Disabilities Act, 2005, S.O. 2005, c. 11", Government of Ontario, last accessed October 13, 2023, https://www.ontario.ca/laws/statute/05a11

Canada

Canada Labour Code

Canadian Human Rights Act

Canadian Charter of Rights and Freedoms

Employment Equity Act

Alberta

Alberta Bill of Rights

Alberta Human Rights Act

Labour Relations Code

Workers' Compensation Act

British Columbia

Declaration on the Rights of Indigenous Peoples Act

Guide Dog and Service Dog Act

Human Rights Code

Labour Relations Code

Manitoba

The Discriminatory Business Practices Act

The Human Rights Code

New Brunswick

Human Rights Act

Newfoundland and Labrador

Human Rights Act

Nova Scotia

An Act Respecting Service Dogs
Human Rights Act
Multiculturalism Act

Ontario

Accessibility for Ontarians with Disabilities Act
Anti-Racism Act
Employment Equity Act
Human Rights Code

Prince Edward Island

Human Rights Act
Pay Equity Act

Quebec

Act Respecting Equal Access to Employment in Public Bodies
Charter of Human Rights and Freedoms

Saskatchewan

The Saskatchewan Employment Act
The Saskatchewan Human Rights Code

Northwest Territories

Human Rights Act

Nunavut
Human Rights Act

Yukon
Human Rights Act

The Tribunals

The two levels of jurisdictions also provide different tribunals to hear cases regarding human rights – the Canadian Human Rights Tribunal and the provincial or territorial human rights tribunal. The Canadian Human Rights Tribunal deals with matters related to the federal government and businesses regulated and registered at the national level. For example, the federal government regulates some employers and service providers; normally, those companies are registered Canada-wide, such as banks and telecommunication companies. Suppose a complaint about human rights is related to those companies. In that case, the complainant will have to go to the Canadian Human Rights Commission to file that complaint instead of going to the provincial or territorial one. The thirteen provincial and territorial human rights offices are:

Alberta Human Rights Commission
British Columbia's Office of the Human Rights Commissioner
Manitoba Human Rights Commission
New Brunswick Human Rights Commission

Newfoundland and Labrador Human Rights Commission
Northwest Territories Human Rights Commission
Nova Scotia Human Rights Commission
Ontario Human Rights Commission
Prince Edward Island Human Rights Commission
Quebec Human Rights and Youth Rights Commission
Saskatchewan Human Rights Commission
Nunavut Human Rights Tribunal
Yukon Human Rights Commission

Every person in Canada has the right to equal treatment without discrimination based on human rights grounds. As a general rule in all the provinces and territories, the human rights grounds include age, ancestry, colour, citizenship, creed, disability, ethnic origin, family status, marital status, place of origin, race, the record of offences, sex, and sexual orientation. However, it depends on the type of human rights case involved; the case may have to be dealt with at the federal or provincial (territorial) level. For example, if the case is related to the employment of a business in one of the following industries or workplaces, then the case will most likely be heard at the federal level:

Air transportation
Banks
Federal Crown corporations
First Nations Band Councils
Grain elevators, feed and seed mills, feed warehouses and grain-seed cleaning plants

Port services, marine shipping, ferries, tunnels, canals, bridges and pipelines (oil and gas) that cross international or provincial borders
Radio and television broadcasting
Railways that cross provincial or international borders
Road transportation services, including trucks and buses that cross provincial or international borders
Telecommunications
Uranium mining and processing and atomic energy
Any business that is vital, essential or integral to the operation of one of the above activities

In addition to the above, all private-sector firms and municipalities in the Northwest Territories, Nunavut and Yukon also fall into the federal jurisdiction. Otherwise, it should fall into the provincial or territorial jurisdiction where the case occurs.

Freedom of Expression

Freedom of expression (or freedom of speech) is not a defence against human rights violations.

In *R. v. Keegstra,*[60] a high school teacher was charged under the Criminal Code with wilfully promoting hatred against an identifiable group by communicating anti-semitic statements to his students. The teacher applied to the Court of Queen's Bench for

[60] 1990 CanLII 24 (SCC), [1990] 3 SCR 697

an order quashing the charge on the ground that the Criminal Code violated his freedom of expression as guaranteed by s. 2(b) of the Canadian Charter of Rights and Freedoms. The Court dismissed his application and found the teacher guilty. The teacher appealed, and the Court of Appeal accepted his argument. The Supreme Court upheld that it is constitutional for the Criminal Code provision to prohibit the wilful promotion of hatred against an identifiable group under the Canadian Charter of Rights and Freedoms.

3. Age

In most jurisdictions in Canada, the Code defines age as 18 years or older. However, in some cases, persons below 18 are also protected from discrimination in some areas. For example, age is defined as age 16 or older in Ontario when dealing with housing issues when they are not living with their parents.

Employment

Stereotypes about older workers are common in our society. Older workers are often unfairly perceived as less committed to their jobs, not energetic, not creative, less productive, unreceptive to change, and unable or costly to be trained. Therefore, some employers may have a preference for the age of their prospective employees or have a mandatory retirement age for their existing employees. Age discrimination is, therefore, a common ground of human rights violations involving employment disputes.

All employers should prevent discrimination by avoiding publishing an advertisement for a job that expresses a limitation, specification, or preference as to age. For example, an employment advertisement that says, "the company is looking for a young and energetic person", shows a preference for age, so it should not be allowed.

In *O'Brien v. Ontario Hydro*,[61] a forty-year-old man alleged that he was not considered for an apprentice electrician position because of his age. Although the employer did hire people in the 40 to 65 age range, they were not hired for its apprenticeship program. The Tribunal concluded that age stereotyping was the proximate cause, and therefore there was discrimination.

In *Air Canada v. Carson*,[62] the Federal Court of Appeal holds that the airline's company policy of not hiring pilots over age 27 is a discriminatory practice under s. 2 of the Canadian Human Rights Act.

Similarly, in *McCreary v. Greyhound Lines of Canada Ltd*,[63] an inter-city bus company had a policy not to hire people over the age of 34 to be their drivers. The Canadian Human Rights Tribunal ruled that such a policy was discriminatory and was not a bona fide requirement, and the company had to cease the discriminatory practice.

All employers should ensure their work environment is discrimination-free, with equal opportunities for older workers.

---

[61] (1981) 2 CHRR D/504 (Ont. Bd. Inq.)
[62] 1985 CanLII 3113 (FCA), [1985] 1 FC 209
[63] 1986 CanLII 82 (CHRT)

In *Kearns v. P. Dickson Trucking Ltd,*[64] the 69-year-old complainant was, by evidence, the best salesman of the company. He was terminated despite his excellent performance, and the reason given suggested that there would no longer be a need for his position. However, his position was not declared redundant and was later filled by a younger person. The Canadian Human Rights Tribunal held that the termination was based solely on age. The complainant was awarded damages for lost wages and special damages for hurt feelings.

In *Silzer v. Chaparral (86) Inc*,[65] the British Columbia Human Rights Tribunal found that an employer discriminated against the 64-year-old complainant on the basis of age (together with a perceived physical or mental disability) when he was not recalled to work after a layoff.

In *Andronik and Boothby v. Guildford Golf and Country Ltd*,[66] the tribunal found that the employer discriminated against an employee by not assigning her certain tasks and subjecting her to an unwanted transfer due to her age. It is discriminatory and a breach of the Code to believe that older people have greater difficulty adapting to technological change and would find it difficult to operate the computer system.

For years, the age for mandatory retirement has been a controversial topic in human rights. In *McKinney v. University of*

---

[64] 1988 CanLII 111 (CHRT)
[65] (1993) 20 C.H.R.R. D/155 (B.C.C.H.R.)
[66] (1993) 21 C.H.R.R. D/400 (B.C.C.H.R.)

Guelph,[67] eight professors and a librarian applied for declarations that the universities' mandatory retirement policies at age 65 were discriminative. They claimed the policies violate s. 15 of the Canadian Charter of Rights and Freedoms, s. 4(1) and s. 9(a) of the Ontario Human Rights Code[68] by not treating persons who attain the age of 65 equally with others.

Section 4(1) of the Code stated, "*Every person has a right to equal treatment with respect to employment without discrimination because of race, ancestry, place of origin, colour, ethnic origin, citizenship, creed, sex, age, record of offences, marital status, family status or handicap*" but Section 9(a) stated, "*except in subsection 4 (1) where "age" means an age that is eighteen years or more and less than sixty-five years*". In other words, people over the age of sixty-four are not protected by the Code.

The Supreme Court of Canada found that the maximum age limit of 65 was prima facie discrimination on the basis of age contrary to Section 15(1) of the Canadian Charter of Rights and Freedoms, which states,

> "*Every individual is equal before and under the law and has the right to the equal protection and equal benefit of*

---

[67] 1990 CanLII 60 (SCC), [1990] 3 SCR 229

[68] "c 53 Human Rights Code, 1981", Osgoode Digital Commons, last accessed October 13, 2023, https://digitalcommons.osgoode.yorku.ca/cgi/viewcontent.cgi?article=2601&context=ontario_statutes

the law without discrimination and, in particular, without discrimination based on race, national or ethnic origin, colour, religion, sex, age or mental or physical disability".

On the other hand, the court also ruled that it was a reasonable limit on the right and hence saved by Section 1 of the Charter, which states, "*... subject only to such reasonable limits prescribed by law as can be demonstrably justified in a free and democratic society*".

Not every province or territory has an upper limit in protecting against age discrimination. Mandatory retirement at the age of 65 was again the core issue in *Dickason v. University of Alberta.*[69] Although the Individual's Rights Protection Act[70] in Alberta did not have a maximum age, the Supreme Court of Canada still ruled that permitting the employer to discriminate against individuals over the age of 64. The Cout held that the policy was reasonable and justifiable under s. 1 of the Canadian Charter of Rights and Freedoms in the circumstances which applied to that retirement scheme.

Similar rulings are found in other cases, such as *Stoffman v. Vancouver General Hospital*[71] and *Cooper v. Canada (Human*

---

69 1992 CanLII 30 (SCC), [1992] 2 SCR 1103

70 "Individual's Rights Protection Act, RSA 1980, c I-2", Canadian Legal Information Institute, last updated November 10, 2020, https://www.canlii.org/en/ab/laws/stat/rsa-1980-c-i-2/latest/rsa-1980-c-i-2.html

71 1990 CanLII 62 (SCC), [1990] 3 SCR 483

Rights Commission).[72] It seems that mandatory retirement at age sixty-five has always been found justifiable by the Supreme Court of Canada. However, with the advancement of society and technology, people's mental and physical health at the age of sixty-five is improving as well.

Why should people be mandatorily retired at 65 when the general health conditions of people in our society are improving? Setting the retirement age at sixty-five by the Code has been reviewed by some provinces. However, the mandatory retirement age may still be allowed and supported by the provincial or territorial human rights code until then.

For example, Section 24(1)(b) of the Ontario Human Rights Code states that *equal treatment with respect to employment is not infringed where the discrimination in employment is for reasons of age, sex, record of offences or marital status if the age, sex, record of offences or marital status of the applicant is a reasonable and bona fide qualification because of the nature of the employment.*[73] Similar provisions in the human rights code may be found in other provinces and territories.

In other words, a government may permit discrimination on the basis of age, where it is a reasonable and bona fide qualification because of the nature of the employment. That is

---

[72] 1996 CanLII 152 (SCC), [1996] 3 SCR 854

[73] "Human Rights Code, R.S.O. 1990, c. H.19", Government of Ontario, last accessed October 13, 2023, https://www.ontario.ca/laws/statute/90h19#BK17

called a bona fide occupational requirement or BFOR defence in discrimination in employment.

In *Ontario Human Rights Commission v. Etobicoke,*[74] several firefighters challenged a mandatory retirement policy to force them to retire at age 60. In a unanimous decision, the Supreme Court of Canada ruled that the retirement of firefighters at age 60 constitutes a violation of the Ontario Human Rights Code because the employer in the case did not discharge the onus of proof necessary to establish that a BFOR justified the early mandatory retirement age.

When delivering the verdict, McIntyre J. set out two tests to determine whether a mandatory retirement scheme is justifiable:

1. It must be imposed honestly, in good faith, and in the belief that such limitation is imposed in the interests of the adequate performance of the work involved with all reasonable dispatch, safety and economy and not for ulterior or extraneous reasons aimed at objectives which could defeat the purpose of the Code.

2. It must be related in an objective sense to the performance of the employment concerned, in that it is reasonably necessary to assure the efficient and economical performance of the job without endangering

---

[74] 1982 CanLII 15 (SCC), [1982] 1 SCR 202

the employee, the fellow employees and the general public.

The two tests were applied in the Supreme Court again in *Large v. Stratford (City)*.[75] In that case, a police officer filed a complaint with the Ontario Human Rights Commission, alleging that the age 60 mandatory retirement policy contravened the 1980 Ontario Human Rights Code on the grounds of age discrimination. Unlike in the case *Ontario Human Rights Commission v. Etobicoke* above, the Supreme Court ruled that the mandatory retirement policy was justified as a BFOR.

The same ruling was found in *Cooper v. Canada (Human Rights Commission)*.[76] A group of pilots alleged that the airline's policy for mandatory retirement at age 60 was discriminative and filed a complaint to the Canadian Human Rights Commission. The Canadian Human Rights Commission dismissed the complaint. The pilots appealed, and the appeal was dismissed by both the Court of Appeal and the Supreme Court.

However, since the Ontario Human Rights Commission amended its Code in 2006, it made mandatory retirement policies illegal for most employers in Ontario. For example, in *Association of Justices of the Peace of Ontario v. Ontario (Attorney General)*,[77] the court ruled that mandatory retirement of justices of the peace at

---

[75] 1995 CanLII 73 (SCC), [1995] 3 SCR 733
[76] 1996 CanLII 152 (SCC), [1996] 3 SCR 854
[77] 2008 CanLII 26258 (ON SC)

the age of 70 violates s. 15(1) the Canadian Charter of Rights and Freedoms.

Goods and Services

In *Ontario (Human Rights Commission) v. Ontario,*[78] the complainant was a 71-year-old, legally blind man. He applied to the provincial Assistive Devices Program (ADP) for financial assistance in purchasing a closed-circuit television magnifier, which would enable him to read and do other tasks involving fine visual acuity. His application was denied as there was an age limit (18 at that time) for funding visual aids. The Court of Appeal ruled that the discriminatory ground of age in the ADP is not protected by the Code as the age restriction is entirely unrelated to the purpose of the program.

In *Talos v. Grand Erie District School Board,*[79] a teacher's extended health, dental and life insurance benefits were terminated when he reached age 65, although he continued working on a full-time basis. The teacher claimed that an exception in the Human Rights Code that permitted employers the discretion to terminate benefits for workers over age 65 infringed his equality rights. The Code gave an exception that the right to equal treatment with respect to employment without discrimination because of age is not infringed by an employee benefit, pension, superannuation,

---

[78] 1994 CanLII 1590 (ON CA)
[79] 2018 HRTO 680 (CanLII)

group insurance plan or fund that complies with the Employment Standards Act. The Tribunal found, however, that the teacher experienced a direct disadvantage on the basis of age and that his rights under s. 15 of the Canadian Charter of Rights and Freedoms had been infringed.

However, in *Zurich Insurance Co v. Ontario (Human Rights Commission)*,[80] the Supreme Court of Canada ruled that the insurance company did not discriminate against the claimant by charging the claimant higher premiums for automobile insurance. The differentiation in automobile insurance rates based on age, sex and marital status was reasonable and bona fide within the meaning of the Code.

Other Issues

In *Law v. Canada (Minister of Employment and Immigration)*,[81] a case regarding the survivor's pension, a 30-year-old claimant was denied survivor's benefits under the Canada Pension Plan. The Supreme Court of Canada ruled that the claimant was not entitled to the survivor's pension when her spouse died simply because of her age (she was 30), which was not discriminative and was justified in a free and democratic society under s. 1 of the Canadian Charter of Rights and Freedoms. The

---

[80] 1992 CanLII 67 (SCC), [1992] 2 SCR 321
[81] 1999 CanLII 675 (SCC), [1999] 1 SCR 497

Court noted that the law did not stereotype, exclude, devalue or demean adults of the claimant's age.

4. Creed

Canadians should be treated the same way, have access to the same opportunities and benefits, and be dealt with equal dignity and respect, regardless of their creed. Creed is not a well-defined term, but the courts and tribunals have often referred to religious beliefs and practices. In some jurisdictions, such as the federal government, the term *religion* is used instead of *creed.* However, several decisions[82] have recognized that the term 'creed' can mean more than religion.

When a rule or policy conflicts with religious practice, the organization has a duty to ensure that the affected individuals are able to observe their religion unless this would cause undue hardship because of cost or health and safety reasons. According to the Ontario Human Rights Commission, unlawful discrimination because of religion can include:

> *Refusing to make an exception to dress codes to recognize religious dress requirements;*
>
> *Refusing to allow individuals to observe periods of prayer at particular times during the day;*

---

[82] *Such as R.C. v. District School Board of Niagara*, 2013 HRTO 1382 (CanLII) and *Rand v. Sealy Eastern Ltd.* (1982), 3 C.H.R.R. D/938 (Ont. Bd. Inq.)

Refusing to permit individuals to take time off to observe a religious holiday.

Employment

In *Bhinder v. Canadian National Railway,*[83] the employer required all persons in its coach yard to wear hard hats. The tribunal ruled that such a policy was discriminating against the complainant, being a Sikh, for religious reasons, and could not wear anything on his head other than a turban.

The Tribunal noted that an employer is obliged to cover the additional risk and liability created by Sikhs whose religion prohibits compliance with hard hat requirements, where there is no basis for a BFOR. That is, where the public or other employees' safety is not jeopardized, and there is no undue hardship placed on the employer either practically or economically. It also ruled that the ensuing risk of increased liability is legitimate, and employers are obliged to accept it. It is because the employer's liability, as determined under the relevant compensation law, is not an undue hardship, and a discriminatory safety policy to minimize that liability is not a BFOR.

In *Yousufi v. Toronto Police Services Board,*[84] the complainant, a non-White person of Afghan descent, was

---

[83] 1981 CanLII 4 (CHRT)
[84] 2009 HRTO 20 (CanLII)

perceived to be of Muslim faith and had experienced harassment. The Tribunal ruled that he was subjected to a poisoned work environment because of his ethnic origin and was discriminated against accordingly.

In *Hadzic v. Pizza Hut*,[85] a Bosnian Serb made death threats to his co-worker, a Bosnian Muslim. The British Columbia Human Rights Tribunal held that the employer was liable for the discrimination against the complainant with respect to conditions of employment based on his creed because its response to the death threats against one of its employees was inadequate.

In another case, the employer was also held liable, although it was not directly involved in the case. In *Asad v. Kinexus Bioinformatics*,[86] a Muslim Canadian citizen was investigated by the Royal Canadian Mounted Police (RCMP) after a co-worker reported him as someone suspected of being involved in the 9/11 attacks. The British Columbia Human Rights Tribunal found that had the complainant not been an Arab Muslim who had immigrated from the middle east, the co-worker would not have acted the way she did. Although it was not the employer who reported the case to the RCMP, the tribunal held that the employer was responsible for discriminatory racial profiling in the workplace by failing to take any actions to address the impact on the complainant.

---

[85] 1999 BCHRT 44 (CanLII)
[86] 2008 BCHRT 293 (CanLII)

In *Qureshi v. G4S Security Services*,[87] the complainant was a young Muslim male who applied for a company's security guard position. The company required all applicants to work on shifts, and the complainant would need approximately one hour off each Friday afternoon to pray. As a result, the complainant was rejected from the recruitment process as soon as the company learned that he had such a need. The Ontario Human Rights Tribunal held that the company discriminated against the complainant on the basis of creed.

In *Dastghib v. Richmond Auto Body and others (No. 2)*,[88] the complainant alleged that his former employer and supervisors discriminated against him in his employment through name-calling. The Tribunal found that the name-calling of the two supervisors did involve ethnic names before and after the US's 9/11 attacks, which would lead to a comparison to a mass murderer, a dictator, or a terrorist. As a result, the Tribunal ruled that there was a prima facie case of discrimination based on the complainant's race, colour, place of origin, political belief and religion.

Employers are obligated to provide accommodations to employees who need the flexibility to fulfill the practice of their religious beliefs.

---

[87] 2009 HRTO 409 (CanLII)
[88] 2007 BCHRT 197 (CanLII)

In *Derksen v. Myert Corps Inc*,[89] an employer dismissed an employee in part for taking an unauthorized day off for religious holy days. The Tribunal found that the employer did not make any effort to accommodate the employee's religious needs. Therefore, it violated the British Columbia Human Rights Code.

In *Shapiro v. Peel (Regional Municipality)*,[90] an employer insisted one of its employees use vacation time, lieu time, or take unpaid leave for religious holidays. Such practice was found to be discriminatory. The Tribunal noted that the employee's proposal to work overtime to make up the time was a reasonable one and could have been accommodated by the employer without undue hardship. The fact that overtime was not available to every employee was not a defence, as accommodation should be individually assessed, and not every employee needs to be accommodated in the same way.

In *Ont. Human Rights Comm. v. Simpsons-Sears*,[91] a lady was employed by a retailer and was periodically required to work Friday evenings and Saturdays as a condition of her employment. Since her religion required strict observance of the Sabbath from sundown Friday to sundown Saturday, she had to accept part-time work to resolve that conflict. The lady complained to the Ontario Human Rights Commission, but the Tribunal, Divisional Court and the Court of Appeal dismissed her complaint. The Supreme Court

---

[89] 2004 BCHRT 60 (CanLII)
[90] (No. 2) (1997), 30 C.H.R.R. D/172 (Ont. Bd. Inq.)
[91] 1985 CanLII 18 (SCC), [1985] 2 SCR 536

found that the employer failed to take reasonable steps to accommodate the employee as they were open to him without undue hardship. The work requirement imposed on all employees for business reasons discriminated against the complainant because compliance required her to act contrary to her religious beliefs and did not affect other members of the employed group. That was discrimination against her based on her creed.

However, the Manitoba Board of Adjudication dismissed a complaint related to religious reasons.[92] The complainant was a Mormon and worked as an accounting clerk for the Mennonite College. She was dismissed two days later when the employer learned that she was not a Mennonite faith member. Since the college expected all teachers, students and staff to interact and ensure a total sense of community, the Statement of Faith was a prerequisite to employment for all staff and faculty. As a result, the college had to terminate the complainant's employment. The Board ruled that the termination of the complainant's job was based on a bona fide and reasonable requirement or qualification for employment in accordance with the Code.

Goods and Services

In *Huang v. 1233065 Ontario,*[93] a senior association revoked the complainant's membership because she was a Falun

---

[92] *Schroen v Steinbach Bible College*, 1999 CanLII 32285 (MB HRC)
[93] 2011 HRTO 825

Gong practitioner. The association referred to Falun Gong as "an evil cult". The Tribunal agreed that *religion is not immune from criticism and that disagreement with or criticism of the tenets of its belief system does not necessarily amount to discrimination.* However, the Tribunal found that the comment referring to Falun Gong as an "evil cult" constitutes discrimination within the meaning of the Code.

In *Modi v. Paradise Fine Foods Ltd,*[94] the complainant was a Christian black African born in Sudan. He went to a halal butchery to purchase meat and had a verbal and physical altercation with the butcher at the store. The Tribunal found that the butcher had initiated the confrontation with inflammatory comments about Sudan's ethnic and religious status, which quickly deteriorated into a physical altercation. The Tribunal concluded that the butcher denied the complainant equal treatment in the provision of a service on the basis of ethnic origin (black African from a non-Muslim culture) and creed (not Muslim).

In *Randhawa v. Tequila Bar & Grill Ltd,*[95] the complainant was denied entry into a nightclub because of his turban. The Tribunal found that the nightclub used video surveillance to identify people waiting in line that it did not want to let in based on their appearance. The complainant was not allowed to get in because of his turban, as the nightclub did not want its patrons to think *"there were a lot of browns inside"*. The Tribunal ruled that

---

[94] 2007 HRTO 12 (CanLII)

[95] 2008 AHRC 3 (CanLII)

the nightclub discriminated against the complainant based on race, religion and ancestry.

In *Williams v. Children's Aid Society of Toronto*,[96] the complainant was a foster parent, and her contract with the service provider was terminated. The Tribunal found that the termination was either directly because of her Christian faith or because of her perceived association with a Christian faith-based youth program. Therefore, it was ruled that the termination of the contract constituted discrimination against the complainant because of her creed.

In *Syndicat Northcrest v. Amselem*,[97] a group of Orthodox Jews bought some units in a co-owned luxury building complex in Montréal. Under the by-laws in the declaration of co-ownership, the balconies of individual units are reserved for the exclusive use of the co-owners of the units to which they are attached. Those co-owners set up "succahs" on their balconies for the purposes of fulfilling the biblically mandated obligation of dwelling in such small enclosed temporary huts during the annual nine-day Jewish religious festival of Succot.

The syndicate of co-ownership requested their removal, claiming that the succahs violated the by-laws. They sent an application for a permanent injunction prohibiting the co-owners from setting up succahs and permitting their demolition. The

---

[96] 2011 HRTO 265 (CanLII)

[97] 2004 SCC 47 (CanLII), [2004] 2 SCR 551

Superior Court granted the application, and the Court of Appeal affirmed the decision. The co-owners appealed to the Supreme Court, and it was found that the succah ritual exists as an article of the Jewish faith, and at least one of the co-owners sincerely believed that dwelling in his own succah is part of his faith, subject to a measure of flexibility when a personal succah is not available.

The Supreme Court noted that freedom of religion is triggered when people demonstrate that they sincerely believe in a practice or belief that has a nexus with religion. As a result, the Supreme Court ruled that the co-owners rights to freedom of religion had been infringed.

In *Ormberg v. Barney's Lounge*,[98] a man entered a bar and ordered a beer. He was told that he would not be served because an unidentified patron found the applicant's shirt to be offensive. On the applicant's shirt was written in one-quarter inch letters, "Hetero is Bettero". He asserted that the words on his shirt were an expression of his deeply felt moral conviction that "the lifestyle choice of heterosexuality is superior to the inferior choice of homosexuality". Therefore, he filed a complaint to the Tribunal saying that he was discriminated against under the prohibited ground of creed. The Tribunal ruled that his deeply held moral convictions cannot legally amount to a claim that engaged the prohibited ground of creed under the Code.

---

[98] 2019 HRTO 21 (CanLII)

In *Loyola High School v. Quebec (Attorney General),*[99] the Minister of Education, Recreation and Sports required a Program on Ethics and Religious Culture, which talked about the beliefs and ethics of different world religions from a neutral and objective perspective, to be taught at all schools. The claimant, a private, English-speaking Catholic high school for boys, brought an application for judicial review of the Minister's decision.

The Superior Court found that the Minister's refusal of an exemption infringed the claimant's right to religious freedom and accordingly granted the application and ordered an exemption. On appeal, the Quebec Court of Appeal ruled that the Minister's decision was reasonable and did not result in any breach of religious freedom. The claimant appealed to the Supreme Court and modified its request to teach the whole program from a Catholic perspective. The Minister insisted that no part of the program could be taught from a Catholic perspective, including Catholic doctrine and ethics. The Supreme Court held that requiring all aspects of the claimant's proposed programs to be taught from a neutral perspective limited freedom of religion. The Court concluded that the Minister's decision infringed the claimant's right to religious freedom under s. 2(a) of the Charter, and could not be justified under s. 1.

In *Adler v. Ontario,*[100] a group of parents sent their children to private religious schools because of religious or conscientious

[99] 2015 SCC 12 (CanLII), [2015] 1 SCR 613
[100] 1996 CanLII 148 (SCC), [1996] 3 SCR 609

beliefs. They sought a declaration that the non-funding of Jewish schools in Ontario was unconstitutional. The Supreme Court of Canada noted that *a multicultural multi-religious society can only work, it is felt, if people of all groups understand and tolerate each other.*

The Supreme Court stated that the real goal of denying funding is not to create a more tolerant society but merely to avoid siphoning any funds from the public school system. As a result, the case was dismissed.

In *Gilbert v. 2093132 Ontario,*[101] a small group of Raelians booked a pub as a venue for their event. They shared a belief system, Raelianism, which has been a "creed" for the Code's purposes. Upon seeing their flyer for the event, the pub's general manager told the organizers that they could not hold the event at the pub and asked them to leave. The general manager also told them the pub did not want to be associated with their "cult". The Tribunal found that the pub's refusal to host a widely-publicized event during one of its busiest times was not discriminatory. However, the general manager's comment constitutes discrimination under the Code.

---

[101] 2011 HRTO 672 (CanLII)

5. Disability

There are different types of disabilities – physical, mental and learning disabilities, mental disorders, hearing or vision disabilities, epilepsy, mental health disabilities and addictions, environmental sensitivities, and other conditions.

Most common diseases and addictions that have been ruled may be the grounds for discrimination based on "disabilities" under the Code. They include but are not limited to acne,[102] alcoholism,[103] allergies and asthma,[104] diabetes,[105] migraine headaches,[106] and obesity.[107]

It is worth noting that the legalization of cannabis for recreational use will not change how human rights apply to the medical use of marijuana. Like other drug use, the Code protects people with disabilities who use cannabis for medical purposes from discriminatory treatments.

---

[102] *De Jong and Horlacher Holdings Ltd* (1989), 10 C.H.R.R. D/6283 (B.C.H.R.C.)

[103] *Milazzo v. Autocar Connaisseur Inc. et al.*, 2003 CHRT 37 (CanLII)

[104] *Wachal v. Manitoba Pool Elevators*, 2000 CanLII 28872 (CHRT)

[105] *Brown v. Canadian Armed Forces*, 1995 CanLII 922 (CHRT)

[106] *Desormeaux v. Ottawa-Carleton Regional Transit*, 2003 CHRT 2 (CanLII)

[107] *Rogal v. Dalgleish* [2000] BCHRTD No. 22; *Dunlop v. Find and Kutzner* (No. 2), 2008 BCHRT 350

Employment

Different courts, tribunals, human rights acts and codes may have different interpretations of the term "disability". The Canadian Human Rights Act defines disability as *any previous or existing mental or physical disability and includes disfigurement and previous or existing dependence on alcohol or a drug.*

The Alberta Human Rights Act[108] defines "mental disability" as *any mental disorder, developmental disorder or learning disorder, regardless of the cause or duration of the disorder*, and "physical disability" as *any degree of physical disability, infirmity, malformation or disfigurement that is caused by bodily injury, birth defect or illness.* The Ontario Human Rights Code[109] has similar definitions with one additional category to cover other cases that may be omitted but fall under the act for worker's compensation.

The human rights law does not include protection for "normal ailments", such as flu or cold, where the effects have no permanence or impairment. In *Newfoundland (Human Rights Commission) v. Health Care Corp. of St. John's,*[110] the complainant alleged that the employer had discriminated against

---

108 "Alberta Human Rights Act", Alberta Queen's Printer, last accessed October 13, 2023, https://www.qp.alberta.ca/documents/Acts/A25P5.pdf

109 "Human Rights Code, R.S.O. 1990, c. H.19", Government of Ontario, last accessed October 13, 2023, https://www.ontario.ca/laws/statute/90h19

110 2001 CanLII 37580 (NL SC)

her on the basis of physical disability when it failed to promote her. The employer's position was that the complainant took about 480 days of sick leave in her 20 years of employment due to serious though unrelated medical conditions, which was the maximum sick leave available. As a result, the employer decided not to promote her because her absences constituted a continuing degree of unreliability, which would jeopardize the leadership and coordinating functions for which she would be responsible. The Tribunal decided that the complainant was not "disabled" as defined by the Human Rights Code.

In *Rutledge v. Fitness One Peter*,[111] a lady with a severe allergy to latex, joined a fitness club after the manager assured her that the facility would be latex-free to accommodate her. After a few months, the lady found latex balloons inside the facility. The new manager told her that he could not ensure that the facility would be latex-free at all times as members sometimes brought balloons into the facility but indicated that she would be made aware of latex in the facility so that she could choose not to come to the facility for a period of time sufficient to allow the contamination to dissipate. However, after a few weeks, she received an e-mail from the new manager advising that a latex balloon had been brought into the facility and that her membership was being cancelled. The Tribunal found that the termination of membership constituted an infringement of the lady's rights under the Code.

---

[111] 2010 HRTO 2039 (CanLII)

A landmark decision delivered by the Supreme Court of Canada[112] involved two cases with two employers and three complainants. The first employer refused to hire two complainants because their pre-employment medical exams revealed an anomaly of the spinal column. The second employer dismissed a police officer because he had Crohn's disease, a type of inflammatory bowel disease.

The human rights commission held that two of the three complainants had no remedy under the Quebec Charter of Human Rights and Freedoms because they did not meet the definition of handicap, as their anomalies did not result in functional limitations. The Court of Quebec ruled that an assessment of a handicap could be objective or purely subjective. It concluded that the first employer's exclusionary policy and its decision not to hire were contrary to s. 10 of Quebec's Charter of Human Rights and Freedoms.

Both cases were appealed and eventually heard in the Supreme Court. The Supreme Court ruled that both employers discriminated against the complainants under the code as a handicap (disability) is not merely a biomedical condition but rather can exist as a perceived limitation or social construct. A person does not have to prove an actual functional inability to perform a job as a precondition to invoking a disability-based

---

[112] *Quebec (Commission des droits de la personne et des droits de la jeunesse) v. Montréal (City); Quebec (Commission des droits de la personne et des droits de la jeunesse) v. Boisbriand (City)*, 2000 SCC 27 (CanLII), [2000] 1 SCR 665

discrimination claim. Therefore, if an employer believes that a person's condition will interfere with business operations and or profitability and, for that reason, dismisses or refuses to hire that person, this perception and consequent treatment can give rise to a finding of discrimination on the basis of a disability under the Code.

The two landmark cases were cited by nearly one thousand cases, including *Chen v. Ingenierie Electro-Optique Exfo*.[113] In *Chen*, the complainant suffered from sciatica, so he had to avoid prolonged standing for more than 20 mins and lifting limited to 15 lbs. When decided sciatica was a "disability" within the meaning of the Code, the Tribunal cited the two cases which ruled that the definition of disability should be interpreted in a broad manner and extends to the actual or perceived possibility that an individual has or may develop a disability in the future.

In *Battlefords and District Co-operative Ltd v. Gibbs*,[114] an employee became disabled as a result of a mental disorder and was unable to work. She received benefits under an insurance policy her employer offered to all its employees. The policy provided a replacement income to all employees as long as their disability prevented them from working until age 65. However, if the disability in question were a mental illness, the replacement income benefit would terminate in two years unless the person with the mental disability remained in a mental institution. Had the

---

[113] 2009 HRTO 1641 (CanLII)

[114] 1996 CanLII 187 (SCC), [1996] 3 SCR 566

disability been physical in nature, her benefits would have continued until age 65, whether or not she was in an institution. As a result, the Supreme Court found that it is discriminatory to limit benefits on the basis of mental disability.

In most jurisdictions, employers, merchants or service providers are required to provide accommodation to employees and customers with disabilities up to the point of undue hardship. However, sometimes, it still depends on the actual situation of the case. In *J.L. v. York Region District School Board*,[115] two students were diagnosed with pes planus, the medical term for flat feet, and requested bussing from the school board. The school board provided bussing for a period of time but stopped. The students filed a complaint with the Tribunal alleging discrimination with respect to goods, services, and facilities because of disability. The Tribunal noted that although pes planus can be a disability, the students did not have a disability, which required accommodation by the school board. The case was dismissed accordingly.

In *McGill University Health Centre (Montreal General Hospital) v. Syndicat des employés de l'Hôpital général de Montréal*,[116] the Supreme Court noted that the duty to accommodate is neither absolute nor unlimited. An employee could not return to work after a three-year absence due to health problems and lost her job by reason of illness. The Supreme Court found there was no discrimination in the employer's refusal to

---

[115] 2013 HRTO 948 (CanLII)
[116] 2007 SCC 4 (CanLII), [2007] 1 SCR 161

continue to employ someone who, after three years of absence due to illness, was still deemed incapable of returning to work by her own doctor.

Goods or Services

In *Eldridge v. British Columbia (Attorney General)*,[117] the complainants were born deaf, so their preferred means of communication was sign language. Medical care in British Columbia did not provide sign language interpretation for people who are deaf or hard of hearing, and its health insurance program did not pay for it. The absence of interpreters impaired their ability to communicate with healthcare providers, thus increasing the risk of misdiagnosis and ineffective treatments. The Supreme Court of Canada ruled that the government must provide sign language interpreters for deaf patients for effective communication in the delivery of medical services to them on equal terms.

In *Ontario (Human Rights Comm.) v. North American Life Assurance Co*,[118] an employee with HIV status was rejected by an insurance company for his claim of long-term disabilities because of his pre-existing medical condition. He filed a complaint with the Ontario Human Rights Commission. However, the Board of Inquiry adjudicator dismissed his case as the adjudicator found the exclusion clause in the insurance plan was not discriminatory

---

117 1997 CanLII 327 (SCC), [1997] 3 SCR 624

118 1995 CanLII 7430 (ON SC)

against his rights. He appealed to the Ontario Court, but his claim was again dismissed. The Court found that his rights were not infringed because there was a reasonable and bona fide reason – his pre-existing medical condition substantially increased the risk under the insurance plan.

In *Moore v. British Columbia (Education)*,[119] a student had severe dyslexia for which he received special education at his public school. In Grade 2, the school district's psychologist recommended that since the student could not get the remedial help he needed at his school, he should attend the local Diagnostic Centre to receive the necessary remediation. The Diagnostic Centre was later closed by the school district, and the student was transferred to a private school.

On behalf of the student, the father of the student filed a complaint to the Tribunal against the school district and the Province on the grounds that the student had been denied a service customarily available to the public under the Code. The Tribunal concluded that there was discrimination against the student and ordered that the family be reimbursed for the tuition costs of the private school. The reviewing judge set aside the Tribunal's decision, finding that there was no discrimination. The Court of Appeal dismissed the appeal, and the father appealed to the Supreme Court.

---

[119] 2012 SCC 61 (CanLII), [2012] 3 SCR 360

The Supreme Court found that the school district failed to provide necessary remediation to the student and discriminated against the student based on his disability under the Code.

In *Council of Canadians with Disabilities v. VIA Rail Canada Inc*,[120] the national rail company was ordered to modify some of their Renaissance cars, both economy coach cars and service cars, to make them personal wheelchair accessible. The Supreme Court found that providing such accommodation to people with disabilities did not impose an undue hardship on the rail company and was reasonable.

---

120 2007 SCC 15 (CanLII), [2007] 1 SCR 650

6. Race and Related Grounds

Racism can be openly displayed in racial jokes, slurs, or hate crimes. It can also be deeply rooted in attitudes, values, and stereotypical beliefs. In some cases, people do not even realize they have these beliefs. Instead, they are assumptions that have evolved over time and have become part of systems and institutions.

Racial discrimination includes those based on race or other related grounds, such as ancestry, ethnicity, religion, or place of origin. It is worth noting that language, on its own, is not a prohibited ground for discrimination under the human rights code. However, jurisprudence recognizes that language can be an element or factor in discrimination based on related grounds such as ancestry, citizenship and creed, ethnic origin, place of origin, and race.

Employment

Canada is a multicultural country, and its workforce has diversified ethnic backgrounds. Employers should be sensitive to racial issues and maintain an environment free of racial discrimination and harassment.

In *Dhillon v. F.W. Woolworth,*[121] a complainant of South Asian ancestry alleged racial epithets by White co-workers were racial discrimination under the Code, which states, "*no person shall discriminate against any employee with regard to any term or condition of employment* …." The Tribunal ruled that the words "term or condition of employment" were broad enough to include the emotional and psychological circumstances of the workplace; hence, racial name-calling and verbal racial harassment constituted discrimination under the Code.

In *Lee v. T.J. Applebee's Food Conglomeration,*[122] the complainant was a Chinese Canadian woman who worked in a bakery in Ontario where racial slurs and stereotypical language were common. None of these remarks were directed specifically to her, but rather to her Black co-workers. Still, the Tribunal found there was indirect racial discrimination. The employer was required to hold a staff seminar to talk about the Code and a work environment free of discriminatory language, with damages awarded to the complainant. The issue of racial name-calling and verbal racial harassment was also considered by the Saskatchewan Human Rights Tribunal in *Lesperance v. Selimos,*[123] and again, it was held that such behaviours caused discrimination.

Insulting or degrading comments or offensive actions aimed at an employee or others in a workplace will create a

---

121 (1982), 3 C.H.R.R. D/743
122 (1987), 9 C.H.R.R. D/4781 (Ont. Bd. Inq.)
123 1996 CanLII 12085 (SK HRT)

poisoned working environment that is discriminatory. The tribunals have held that a poisoned environment is based on the nature of the comments or conduct and its impact on the individual, but not on the number of times the behaviour occurs.[124] A single comment or conduct "*that is known or ought reasonably to be known to be unwelcome*" sufficiently severe or substantial can create a poisoned environment.

In *Payne v. Otsuka Pharmaceuticals Co Ltd*,[125] a pharmaceutical company rejected a Black candidate for a job position after meeting her. The employer was visibly shocked and turned her down flat without asking about her qualifications. When asked what was wrong, the employer implied that it would be bad for the company's image to hire a Black person as their receptionist. The Tribunal concluded that the complainant was rejected because she was Black and held the company liable accordingly. The Tribunal also held the conference organizers liable for assisting the pharmaceutical company in locating other individuals without properly investigating the complainant's allegations of racial discrimination.

In *Wong v. Ottawa Board of Education*,[126] a teacher of Chinese descent was on a surplus list partly because of the limited types of extra-curricular activities he could undertake. The school principal took a narrow view of activities that could be qualified as

---

[124] Such as *Dhanjal v. Air Canada* 1996 CanLII 2385 (CHRT)
[125] 2001 CanLII 26231 (ON HRT)
[126] (No. 2) (1993), 23 C.H.R.R. D/37 (Ont. Bd.Inq.)

"extra-curricular". As a result, the activities that, for cultural reasons, the Chinese teacher would be unlikely to undertake were included, while legitimate activities that he would be more disposed to engage in were excluded. The Tribunal held that the narrow view of extra-curricular activities operated in a discriminatory fashion.

In *Sandhu v. Regional Municipality of Peel Police Services Board*,[127] a South Asian-Canadian police officer was denied the opportunity for promotion into the senior ranks. The Tribunal ruled out the lack of supervisory experience and poor performance as reasons why the complainant was not promoted and ruled that the police discriminated against him on the basis of his race.

In *Smith v. Ontario (Human Rights Commission)*,[128] the complainant was a Black part-time employee of an auto shop. After a few years, he was dismissed. Although the Tribunal found that he was subjected to a poisoned workplace, it was ruled that the termination was not because of race or colour. The Tribunal noted,

> "*Why would the very people who hired him, who were impressed by him, who promoted him, and who accommodated his school schedule in terms of working hours, suddenly make a decision against him based on his race?*"

---

[127] 2014 HRTO 1394 (CANLII), 2017 HRTO 1221 (CanLII)
[128] 2005 CanLII 2811 (ON SCDC)

The complainant appealed, and the Divisional Court recognized that as a common myth. The Tribunal inappropriately focused on the motivation of the employer, which did not properly form part of the analysis of whether racial discrimination occurred. The Court found that two higher-ranking white employees were punished less severely than the complainant for infractions that were arguably more serious than those committed by the complainant, hence ruling that race was a factor in the termination of the complainant's employment.

In *Froman v. TJX Canada*,[129] the complainant was the only Caucasian employee in her department of 17 people, the majority being East Asian. She alleged that her employer discriminated against her because of her race because the management refused to let her change the time of her daily break. She told her employer that she wanted a quieter break period so that she could read and have quiet personal time and sought accommodation, but conceded that she had no special need arising from a Code ground. The Tribunal dismissed the case as the complainant had no evidence to support her allegation that the refusal of her request to switch break times was because of her race.

[129] 2013 HRTO 1191 (CanLII)

Housing

A dispute between a tenant in a basement apartment and his landlord was caused by racial discrimination.[130] The Tribunal found that the landlord's discriminatory conduct consisted of shouting racial epithets, screaming invectives at the tenant, and stomping on the ceiling of his apartment. As a result, the Tribunal held that she violated the tenant's right to reasonable occupation of his apartment because of his race.

In *Rennie v. 7892535 Canada Inc,*[131] a landlord asked her contractor to act as her temporary property manager after the property manager resigned. The new property manager rejected the complainant's rental application, and the Tribunal found that race and colour were a factor in his not getting the apartment. Although there was no discriminatory conduct on the landlord's part, she is liable for paying the compensation for the complainant's injury to dignity.

In *Gregory v. Donauschwaben Park Waldheim Inc,*[132] a seller rejected a buyer to purchase its recreational property inside a park because the buyer was not able to speak German. The park owner was a non-profit society whose objectives were to foster and preserve the culture and heritage of Danube Swabians. As a result, the sale of the recreational property within its park would only be approved by the company if the purchaser were German-speaking.

---

[130] *Fuller v. Daoud*, 2001 CanLII 26227 (ON HRT)
[131] 2020 HRTO 239 (CanLII)
[132] (1990), 13 C.H.R.R. D/505 (Ont. Bd. Inq.)

The Tribunal held that linguistic and ethnic restrictions on purchasing the property were justified under the Ontario Code, which allows fraternal or social organizations serving an identifiable group to limit services or facilities to persons belonging to that group.

In *Commission des droits de la personne et des droits de la jeunesse v. Quévillon,*[133] the complainant was a lady, whose husband was an Arab, of Moroccan origin. The landlord refused to rent her property to the complainant, and the Tribunal found that there was sufficient evidence to conclude that the landlord's decision was influenced by a preoccupation with skin colour and various stereotypes about immigrants and dark-skinned people.

Goods and Services

Peel Law Association v. Pieters[134] is a case involving two lawyers and an articling student; all are Black. During a break from a proceeding at a courthouse, they went to the lawyer's lounge operated by the local law association with some of the other lawyers involved in the proceeding. According to the lounge's policy, only lawyers and law students were permitted to use it, and there were signs to indicate that. The lounge administrator approached the trio and asked them to produce identification to show they were lawyers or law students. She did not ask to see the

133 1999 CanLII 5 (QC TDP)
134 2013 ONCA 396 (CanLII)

identification of anyone else in the lounge. The Court of Appeal found that the association had infringed their rights under the Code to equal treatment with respect to services, goods, and facilities without discrimination because of race and colour.

In *McCarthy v. Kenny Tan Pharmacy Inc*,[135] a Black lady shopped at a drugstore and was stopped by an employee of the drugstore. The employee confronted the lady and searched her backpack because the employee believed that the lady was trying to shoplift products. The employee did not find any products in the lady's backpack and did not apologize to her. Such action that deviated from normal practice was found by the Tribunal a case of race discrimination.

In *Alibhai v. Tequila Bar & Grill Ltd*,[136] the complainant, a visible non-Caucasian, was denied entry by a nightclub and alleged that he was discriminated against based on his race. The nightclub had an age policy that only allowed people over 25 to enter. Since the nightclub had videotapes to support that there was a diverse crowd inside the nightclub, the Tribunal found that their age policy was not discriminatory. The case was dismissed.

In *R. v. Williams*[137], the accused was an aboriginal charged with robbery. The Supreme Court found that the trial judge refused to permit the accused to challenge jurors during the jury selection process and did not warn the jury to be aware of or to disregard

---

[135] 2015 HRTO 1303 (CanLII)

[136] 2008 AHRC 11 (CanLII)

[137] 1998 CanLII 782 (SCC), [1998] 1 SCR 1128

any bias or prejudice that they might feel towards the accused as a native person. The Supreme Court accepted that there was widespread prejudice against aboriginal people in the community, and the judge's refusal for the accused to challenge jurors violated s.15 of the Charter that "*every individual is equal before and under the law and has the right to the equal protection and equal benefit of the law without discrimination*". The accused's appeal was allowed.

In *DesRosiers v. Manhas*,[138] the complainants were two aboriginal women. They paid a deposit to a property owner to rent a house for two years. When they met the owner's wife, she stated she did not rent to "*Indians*" and made further disparaging comments such as "*all you people are drunks*". The Tribunal ruled that the owner's wife discriminated against the two women under the Code.

---

[138] 2000 BCHRT 23 (CanLII)

7. Sex and Related Grounds

When same-sex marriage was illegal in Canada, there were cases ruled by the tribunals that spouses and marital status definitions limited to opposite-sex couples were discriminatory.[139] The Supreme Court of Canada also ruled that the opposite-sex definition of "spouse" violated s. 15(1) of the Charter.[140] After same-sex marriage became legal in Canada in 2005, the issues around same-sex couples[141] have significantly been reduced. However, sex and gender-related discrimination are still possible, and we have to be careful about those issues, especially sexual orientation.

Employment

In *Chapdelaine v. Air Canada*,[142] the complainants possessed all of the qualifications necessary to be a pilot at the times they applied but were rejected by the airline because they failed to meet the minimum height requirement of five feet and six inches. Such discrimination based on their height was ruled under

---

139 Such as *Leshner v. Ontario* (2) (1992), 16 C. H. R. R. D/ 184

140 *M. v. H.*, 1999 CanLII 686 (SCC), [1999] 2 SCR 3

141 Such as cases *Egan v. Canada*, 1995 CanLII 98 (SCC), [1995] 2 SCR 513 and *Halpern v. Canada (Attorney general)*, 2003 CanLII 26403 (ON CA)

142 1987 CanLII 102 (CHRT)

the Code, as it was a discriminatory practice on the grounds of sex. The reasoning of the Tribunal was that over 82% of females in Canada between 20 and 29 years of age were shorter than five feet and six inches, while only 11% of men in the same age category were less than that height. Therefore, the minimum height policy would disqualify 82% of all such women but only 11% of all such men from becoming a pilot.

In *Brooks v. Canada Safeway Ltd,*[143] an employer provided disability benefits of twenty-six weeks paid leave to its employees, but pregnant employees were subject to exclusion from coverage during the period commencing the tenth week prior to the expected week of delivery and ending with the sixth week after the week of delivery. The pregnant employees filed complaints to the Human Rights Commission, but the adjudicator dismissed the claims. The Court of Queen's Bench and the Court of Appeal upheld the adjudicator's decisions, and the complainant appealed to the Supreme Court.

The Supreme Court found that the Court of Appeal relied on the decision of another case, *Bliss v. Attorney General of Canada,*[144] to support its finding that the discrimination was not under the Code because the complainants were pregnant and not because they were women. However, the Supreme Court noted that *Bliss* reached the opposite conclusion, which *is inconsistent with*

---

[143] 1989 CanLII 96 (SCC), [1989] 1 SCR 1219
[144] 1978 CanLII 25 (SCC), [1979] 1 SCR 183

the Court's approach to interpreting human rights legislation taken in subsequent cases and should no longer be followed.

In *Charbonneau v. Atelier Salon & Spa,*[145] the complainant quit her job in Ontario as she planned to go to Florida. After finding out she was pregnant, she asked the employer to rehire her, but it was rejected. The Tribunal found that pregnancy was a factor that contributed to the employer's decision not to rehire her, which was discriminatory under the Code.

The case *Bickell v. The Country Grill*[146] is about the termination of employment during pregnancy. A lady's job as a waitress was terminated by her employer during her pregnancy. The reason the employer gave was that she was "too big to do the job". The Tribunal ruled that the employer discriminated against the complainant based on sex. The employer was required to pay the complainant $15,000.00 as compensation for injury to dignity, feelings, and self-respect. The whole management team was required to take a human rights course from the Ontario Human Rights Commission.

According to the policy of the Ontario Human Rights Commission, "pregnancy" includes the fact that a woman is pregnant, was pregnant, or is planning or trying to conceive. It also includes abortions, miscarriages, complications arising from the pregnancy, or miscarriage.

---

[145] 2010 HRTO 1736 (CanLII)

[146] 2011 HRTO 1333 (CanLII)

Sometimes, employers may have to provide accommodations to their employees to deal with sex-related issues like disabilities-related issues. In *Purres v. London Athletic Club (South) Inc*,[147] the complainant was a pregnant woman working as a customer service associate at a fitness club. As she experienced swelling in her feet and pain in her legs, her doctor advised her to avoid prolonged standing and would benefit from sitting and standing alternatively. The management rejected the idea of placing a stool or chair behind the counter for the complainant, saying it was unsafe because the complainant could be knocked off by other employees passing by in the narrow space behind. The Tribunal rejected that argument and found the employer discriminated against the complainant as they failed to accommodate a pregnant woman's needs.

However, the employees must ensure their employer knows their need for accommodation. In *Chappell v. Securitas Canada Limited*,[148] one of the allegations that the complainant made was that the Union, when arranged for a meeting, did not accommodate her properly regarding her breastfeeding needs, which discriminated against her based on sex. The Tribunal found that the complainant did not make an effort to make the Union aware that the location of the meeting would conflict with her breastfeeding plans but just assumed that the Union was aware that she continued to breastfeed. However, the issue last arose more than one year ago. The case was dismissed.

---

[147] 2012 HRTO 1758 (CanLII)

[148] 2012 HRTO 874 (CanLII)

Goods or Services

In *Trinity Western University v. British Columbia College of Teachers*,[149] the British Columbia College of Teachers refused to approve a teacher education program offered by a private institution that required its students to sign a "Community Standards" document prohibiting homosexual behaviour. The College's decision was made on the basis that it was contrary to the public interest for the College to approve a teacher education program that appeared to follow discriminatory practices. While the Supreme Court ruled that the College should approve the program, it also stated that the pluralistic nature of society and the extent of diversity in Canada are important elements that future teachers must understand. There is a need to respect and promote minority rights.

In *Hall (Litigation guardian of) v. Powers*,[150] same-sex marriage was not legal in Ontario then. A student attending Grade 12 at a Catholic high school was denied permission by his high school to bring his boyfriend to the school prom. The Ontario Superior Court had to balance the student's right to be free from discrimination on the basis of his sexual orientation under s. 15 of the Charter with the right to freedom of religion of the school. The Court recognized a diversity of opinion within the Catholic community with regard to homosexuality and found that the restrictions imposed on the student's rights were not defensible

---

[149] 2001 SCC 31 (CanLII), [2001] 1 SCR 772

[150] 2002 CanLII 49475 (ON SC)

under the Charter. The Court granted an interlocutory injunction restraining the school from preventing the student's attendance with his boyfriend at the prom.

In *Brockie v. Brillinger (No. 2)*,[151] a printer refused to provide services to a charity that promotes lesbian and gay people's interests because his religion believed that homosexual conduct was sinful. It is a matter of protecting the printer's right to freedom of religion versus protecting the lesbian and gay group's freedom of sexual orientation. The Tribunal ordered the printer to provide the same printing services to lesbian and gay people that they provide to other members of the public. The printer appealed, and the Court added to the Tribunal's order, "*shall not require the printer to print material of nature which could reasonably be considered to be in direct conflict with the core elements of his religious beliefs or creed*".

In *M.D.R. v. Ontario (Deputy Registrar General)*,[152] two lesbian parents whose children were conceived through reproductive technology sought to have the names of both co-mothers listed on the Statement of Live Birth but were rejected. It was because the Vital Statistics Act (VSA) only permitted the listing of one mother and one father. The Court ruled that the birth registry provisions of the VSA were declared invalid because they had the effect of infringing the mothers' right to be protected

---

[151] 2002 CanLII 63866 (ON SCDC) and *Ontario (Human Rights Commission) v. Brockie*, 2004 CanLII 16323 (ON CA)
[152] 2006 CanLII 19053 (ON SC)

against discrimination based on sex under s. 15 of the Charter. Both women could register as the child's mother. In a similar case,[153] the child's biological father was also allowed to register as one of the three parents on the documents.

In *Nichols v. M.J.*,[154] a marriage commissioner refused to perform a marriage between two gay men. His reason for refusion was that he held a sincere and genuine religious belief, so he was unable to solemnize a marriage for a same-sex couple. The Tribunal ruled that the marriage commissioner discriminated against the men based on the prohibited grounds of their sexual orientation. The marriage commissioner appealed to the Superior Court, but the appeal was dismissed.

---

[153] *A.A. v. B.B.*, 2007 ONCA 2 (CanLII)
[154] 2009 SKQB 299 (CanLII)

8. Other Grounds

Some issues may not be as common as the grounds in the previous chapters, and some issues may partially fall into the Code as a ground of discrimination, such as a Record of Offences when it is related to employment. They are included in this chapter, and most of them are employment-related.

Family Status

> "*...those who bear children and benefit society as a whole thereby should not be economically or socially disadvantaged seems to bespeak the obvious*".

The above is a statement noted by the Supreme Court of Canada in one of the landmark cases involving human rights.[155] Discrimination based on family or marital status is still a challenge in Canada.

In *Saskatchewan (Human Rights Commission) v. Prince Albert Elks Club Inc*,[156] a woman was hired as a club manager. She was summarily fired approximately two weeks later by the

---

[155] *Brooks v. Canada Safeway Ltd.*, 1989 CanLII 96 (SCC), [1989] 1 SCR 1219

[156] 2002 SKCA 106 (CanLII)

board of the club after they learned she was married to a convicted murderer. The Court of Appeal for Saskatchewan ruled that the woman was refused continued employment because of marital discrimination.

In *Williamson v. Saskatchewan Forest Products Corp,*[157] a man applied for a job that he was well qualified for, but the employer rejected him simply because his wife was also working at the same plant. The employer had a corporate policy that spouses of employees working at the plant would not be hired. The Tribunal found that the employer discriminated against the man because of his marital status.

In *York Condominium v. Dudnik,*[158] a condominium corporation's bylaw barred families with children younger than 18 from occupying the condominium units. The complainants were individuals with children who were residing in the building or wanted to purchase a unit in the building. The Tribunal found that such a bylaw was in breach of the Code. "Adults only" condominium complex is not allowed.

Record of Offences

Under the Canadian Human Rights Act, discrimination based on a conviction for an offence for which a pardon has been

---

[157] 1993 CanLII 9120 (SK HRT)
[158] (Div. Ct.), 1991 CanLII 7224 (ON SC)

granted is not allowed. In Ontario, discrimination based on a record of offences is not allowed in employment except for bona fide requirements. However, different legislative provisions in various jurisdictions have led to varying results of precedents.

In *McKenzie v. Ontario (Government Services)*,[159] the complainant applied for a government job but was refused due to his background check. The complainant had never been convicted of a crime because all charges against him were either dropped or for which he received a discharge. However, the Ministry of Government Services rejected him because of those charges. The Tribunal ruled that the code does not apply to someone who was charged with a criminal offence but does not have a criminal record.

Similarly, in *Hussey v. Big Brothers Big Sisters of Peterborough Incorporated*,[160] the complainant was hired by her employer on the condition of providing a clean criminal reference check and vulnerable sector screening clearance before commencing employment. The complainant failed to do it before starting her job and later found that she had a conviction before. The employer dismissed her before she could receive her pardon. The Tribunal ruled that the Code only protects someone with a pardon and does not protect someone simply charged with an offence.

---

[159] 2010 HRTO 1186 (CanLII)
[160] 2013 HRTO 16 (CanLII)

On the other hand, the British Columbia Human Rights Tribunal extended the protection to persons merely charged with an offence even though the explicit protection in their Code is for someone convicted of an offence.[161] In that case, the complainant did not have a criminal record but was dismissed by her employer because of a criminal act she committed when she worked for the previous employer. The Tribunal decided that it was under the Code mainly based on the *Supreme Court of Canada, which has repeatedly said that human rights legislation should be given a large and liberal interpretation* and that the Supreme Court of British Columbia also said that the rehabilitation of persons convicted of criminal offences is to be encouraged through the application of human rights legislation.[162]

Height and Weight

Some employers may have height and weight requirements for their jobs. Based on the situation, they may be the minimum or the maximum limits. In *Chapdelaine*, the case was about a minimum height requirement as a condition to be a pilot. However, such standards for height and weight would unintentionally screen out certain applicants, such as women and racialized persons. As a result, the Ontario Human Rights Commission amended its Code to allow such discrimination only if:

---

[161] *Clement v. Jackson and Abdulla*, 2006 BCHRT 411 (CanLII)

[162] *Woodward Stores Ltd v. McCartney* (1983), 4 C.H.R.R. D/1325, at para. 11467

1. it was adopted for a purpose that is rationally connected to the function being performed

2. it was adopted in good faith, in the belief that it is needed to fulfill the purpose,

3. it is reasonably necessary to accomplish its purpose, in the sense that the person cannot be accommodated without undue hardship.[163]

The crucial issue is to determine whether the employer has shown that accommodation has been provided up to the point of undue hardship.

For example, in *Ede v. Canadian Armed Forces,*[164] the Tribunal held that a minimum height requirement was not discriminatory under the Code as the redesign and manufacture of vehicles and equipment to fit a shorter body height was not feasible. The same argument was also used by the Tribunal in *Bhinder.*

---

[163] Guide to Your Rights and Responsibilities Under the Code_2013, Ontario Human Rights Commission, , last accessed October 13, 2023, http://www3.ohrc.on.ca/sites/default/files/Guide%20to%20Your%20Rights%20and%20Responsibilities%20Under%20the%20Code_2013.pdf

[164] 1990 CanLII 6576 (CHRT)

Canadian Experience

It is worth noting that in Ontario, requiring "Canadian experience" has been identified by the Ontario Human Rights Commission as a discriminatory barrier for newcomers to Canada. Employers may not ask questions regarding an applicant's work experience in Canada unless the "Canadian experience" is a bona fide requirement for the job. Although other provinces do not have an equivalent policy to call the use of "Canadian experience" discriminatory on human rights grounds, such a requirement may still be discriminatory unless the employer can prove it is necessary. Consequently, the employer may be exposed to liability for general damages for human rights violations.

There have been legal challenges to qualification rules for foreign-trained doctors in different provinces. In *Jamorski v. Ontario (Attorney General),*[165] the Court of Appeal ruled that different internship requirements for graduates of unaccredited medical schools did not infringe s. 15 of the Canadian Charter of Rights and Freedoms. On the other hand, the British Columbia Human Rights Tribunal ruled that foreign-trained doctors were discriminated against on the basis of place of origin by a requirement of the College of Physicians and Surgeons of British Columbia that they have an additional year of post-graduate training in order to be eligible for registration.[166]

---

165 1988 CanLII 4738 (ON CA)

166 *Bitonti et al v. The College of Physicians and Surgeons of BC et al*, 1999 BCHRT 63 (CanLII)

Canadian Citizenship

In *Andrews v. Law Society of British Columbia,*[167] the complainant was a permanent resident in Canada who met all the requirements for admission to the British Columbia bar except that of Canadian citizenship. He applied for a declaration that the requirement of Canadian citizenship violated s. 15(1) of the Canadian Charter of Rights and Freedoms. His case was dismissed at trial but allowed on appeal. Eventually, the case went to the Supreme Court. The Supreme Court noted *a rule that bars an entire class of persons from certain forms of employment solely on the grounds of a lack of citizenship status and without consideration of educational and professional qualifications or the other attributes or merits of individuals in the group, infringes s. 15 equality rights.* The Court also noted that the restriction of access to the profession to citizens is over-inclusive.

Positive Discrimination

Some kinds of 'positive discrimination' are allowed under the Code. For example, many merchants offer seniors over the age of 65 a discount, which is permitted as positive discrimination under the Code. The rationale is partially based on the fact that people over 65 have historically been subjected to discrimination. The same logic applies to seniors-only housing. However, caution

167 1989 CanLII 2 (SCC), [1989] 1 SCR 143

must be made when setting up such policies, especially if it is not for seniors but for other categories based on other grounds.

Authority of the Canadian Human Rights Tribunal

It is also worth noting that there is a limitation of the Canadian Human Rights Tribunal. In *Canada (Canadian Human Rights Commission) v. Canada (Attorney General),*[168] the Supreme Court of Canada heard a case that dealt with the authority of the Canadian Human Rights Tribunal.

A woman filed a complaint to the Tribunal alleging that the Canadian Forces had discriminated against her on the grounds of sex contrary to the provisions of the Canadian Human Rights Act. The Tribunal concluded that her complaint of sexual harassment was substantiated in part, and she was awarded $4,000 to compensate for "suffering in respect of feelings or self-respect". The complainant applied for legal costs. The Tribunal determined that it had the authority to order costs pursuant to s. 53(2)(c) and (d) of the Act and awarded her $47,000 in this regard.

The Federal Court upheld the Tribunal's decision on its authority to award costs. The Federal Court of Appeal allowed an appeal of this decision and held that the Tribunal had no authority to make a costs award. The Supreme Court found that there is no reasonable interpretation of the relevant statutory provisions to

---

[168] 2011 SCC 53 (CanLII), [2011] 3 SCR 471

support the view that the Tribunal may award legal costs to successful complainants. That is, the Canadian Human Rights Tribunal does not have the power to award legal fees. This ruling may create a disincentive for lawyers to represent complainants who do not have the money to cover legal fees upfront.

9. Indigenous People

There are over 250 million Indigenous people around the world[169] , and they face eviction from their ancestral lands, being denied the opportunity to equal access to services, goods and justice. Indigenous people are often marginalized and face discrimination in countries' legal systems. They may not express their culture, be under physical attacks, and be treated discriminatorily. Most countries have legislation to protect Indigenous people and assist them in housing, education and other areas.

UNDRIP

In 2007, the United Nations General Assembly adopted the United Nations Declaration on the Rights of Indigenous Peoples (UNDRIP) by a majority of 144 states in favour, four votes against (Australia, Canada, New Zealand, and the United States).[170] UNDRIP addresses individual and collective rights, cultural rights and identity, and rights to education, health, employment,

[169] "Indigenous peoples", Wikipedia, last accessed October 13, 2023, https://en.wikipedia.org/wiki/Indigenous_peoples

[170] "United Nations Declaration on the Rights of Indigenous Peoples", United Nations, last accessed October 13, 2023, https://www.un.org/development/desa/indigenouspeoples/declaration-on-the-rights-of-indigenous-peoples.html

language, and others. It protects Indigenous peoples' rights, including on issues relating to land, culture, identity, religion, language, health, education, governance and community.

Canada issued a Statement of Support[171] in 2010, endorsing the principles of UNDRIP. In 2016, the Minister of Indigenous and Northern Affairs announced that Canada is now a full supporter of the declaration without qualification. UNDRIP is the most comprehensive instrument on the rights of Indigenous peoples all over the world. It establishes a universal framework of minimum standards for the Indigenous peoples' survival, dignity, and well-being. It elaborates on existing Canadian human rights laws that apply to Indigenous peoples' specific situations.

In *Canada (Human Rights Commission) v. Canada (Attorney General)*,[172] the complainants filed a complaint with the Canadian Human Rights Commission. They alleged that the Government of Canada underfunded child welfare services for on-reserve First Nations children. The Government of Canada funds child welfare services for First Nations children living on reserves, while the provinces fund child welfare services for all other Aboriginal and non-Aboriginal children. The Tribunal held that for the complainants to establish adverse differential treatment under

---

[171] "ARCHIVED - Canada's Statement of Support on the United Nations Declaration on the Rights of Indigenous Peoples", Indigenous and Northern Affairs Canada, last accessed October 13, 2023, https://www.aadnc-aandc.gc.ca/eng/1309374239861/1309374546142

[172] 2012 FC 445 (CanLII)

the Canadian Human Rights Act, a comparison had to be made between the child welfare services provided by the Government of Canada to First Nations children living on-reserve and similar services provided to others by the same service provider. According to the Tribunal, the Act does not permit a comparison between two different service providers' services to two different sets of recipients. The case was dismissed by the Tribunal.

The Federal Court noted that the Supreme Court of Canada had recognized the relevance of international human rights law in interpreting domestic legislation such as the Canadian Human Rights Act. International instruments such as the UNDRIP may also inform the contextual approach to statutory interpretation. As a result, the Court found that the Tribunal erred in failing to provide any reasons as to why the complaint could not proceed under the Act and erred in interpreting subsection 5(b) of the Act as requiring an identifiable comparator group in every case in order to establish adverse differential treatment in the provision of services.

The complaint[173] was heard again, and the Tribunal noted that Canada has a positive obligation towards "all First Nations children" regardless of Indian Act status or eligibility for Indian Act status. The Tribunal found Canada's definition and implementation of its principle to be narrow and inadequate,

---

[173] *First Nations Child & Family Caring Society of Canada et al. v. Attorney General of Canada (representing the Minister of Indigenous and Northern Affairs Canada)*, 2020 CHRT 20 (CanLII)

resulting in service gaps, delays, and denials for First Nations children. All the relevant authorities were ordered to consult to generate potential eligibility criteria for First Nations children under the current principle.

In *Watson v. Canada*,[174] the Federal Court noted that although Canada has endorsed UNDRIP and the Principles may be perceived as a positive public policy step towards reconciliation, neither UNDRIP nor the Principles can change or overturn the details set out in Canadian statute. UNDRIP is just a non-binding United Nations resolution supported by Canada as a political commitment. UNDRIP and its Principles are not legally binding on the Canadian government. Still, they might be used to aid in interpreting Canadian domestic law.

The Indian Act[175] has long been controversial legislation in Canada. For example, before an amendment was made in 1951, it was illegal for First Nations people to gather in groups of more than three, leave the reserve without a pass, hire a lawyer, own property, and practice their culture.

Until the Act was amended in 1985, First Nations women's legal status would lose their Indian Status when they married a non-status man. All the children in those marriages would also not be entitled to Indian Status. Before the amendment, aboriginal women would also lose their status if their husbands died or

---

174 2020 FC 129 (CanLII)

175 "Indian Act", Government of Canada, last accessed October 13, 2023, https://laws-lois.justice.gc.ca/eng/acts/i-5/FullText.html

abandoned them, and they were also banned from voting and running in Chief and Council elections.

Still, the Indian Act is believed to be unfair to the Indigenous people. The Assembly of First Nations National Chief called on the federal government to repeal the Indian Act in 2011,[176] but the government showed no response. Hopefully, with the government's support in UNDRIP, there will be a reform in the legislation regarding First Nations people soon.

On the other hand, section 67 of the Canadian Human Rights Act prevented people from filing discrimination complaints resulting from the application of the Indian Act. During that time, discrimination complaints could not be brought against the Government of Canada or First Nations governments. As section 67 was repealed in 2008, the Canadian Human Rights Act now applies to the Government of Canada and the First Nations governments.

Creed

Since Indigenous peoples may not identify their spiritual beliefs as a religion, some jurisdictions (such as Ontario) use the Creed to include Indigenous Spirituality under human rights

---

[176] "Background: The Indian Act", CBC, last updated July 14, 2011, https://www.cbc.ca/news/canada/background-the-indian-act-1.1056988

protection. Several provisions in UNDRIP directly relate to rights associated with practicing Indigenous Spirituality, including but not limited to the following:[177]

Article 12(1): Indigenous peoples have the right to manifest, practise, develop and teach their spiritual and religious traditions, customs and ceremonies; the right to maintain, protect, and have access in privacy to their religious and cultural sites; the right to the use and control of their ceremonial objects; and the right to the repatriation of their human remains.

Article 25: Indigenous peoples have the right to maintain and strengthen their distinctive spiritual relationship with their traditionally owned or otherwise occupied and used lands, territories, waters and coastal seas and other resources and to uphold their responsibilities to future generations in this regard.

Article 34: Indigenous peoples have the right to promote, develop and maintain their institutional structures and their distinctive customs, spirituality, traditions, procedures, practices and, in the cases where they exist, juridical systems or customs, in accordance with international human rights standards.

In *Smith v. Mohan (No. 2)*,[178] an Indigenous woman rented a basement apartment. She practiced smudging as a regular

---

[177] "Resolution adopted by the General Assembly on 13 September 2007", United Nations, last accessed October 13, 2023, https://undocs.org/A/RES/61/295

[178] 2020 BCHRT 52 (CanLII)

spiritual practice, which was also a part of her connection to and expression of her Indigenous identity. After his attempts to evict her for cause failed, the landlord refused to accept her rent payments. The Tribunal ruled that a policy that prohibits an Indigenous tenant from smudging entirely due to concerns about "nuisance" or "property damage" would adversely impact Indigenous persons with their protected characteristics in and of itself. Indigenous women's spiritual practices are protected by religion as a protected characteristic.

The Challenges

According to different information sources, over half of Inuit persons living in Inuit Nunangat report food insecurity,[179] nearly half of the children in foster care are Indigenous,[180] more than one-third of housing units on First Nations reserves are in

[179] "Study: Food insecurity among Inuit living in Inuit Nunangat, 2012", Statistics Canada, last updated February 1, 2017, https://www150.statcan.gc.ca/n1/daily-quotidien/170201/dq170201a-eng.pdf

[180] "Insights on Canadian Society", Statistics Canada, last updated April 13, 2016, https://www150.statcan.gc.ca/n1/pub/75-006-x/2016001/article/14547-eng.htm

need of major repairs,[181] and a quarter of federal inmates are Indigenous.[182]

The Indigenous peoples in Canada face difficult situations and require suitable programs and government policies to assist them. Like all Canadians, the Indigenous peoples have the right to have the opportunity to make the life they want for themselves and their families. They deserve the right to live with health, safety, well-being, security, and access to human rights and justice. Among them, Indigenous females face more challenges than males, as historically, Indigenous women have a lower social status in their communities.

In *Tanner v. Gambler First Nation*,[183] the complainant was an Aboriginal woman registered as an "Indian" pursuant to the Indian Act. She was born a member of the Sagkeeng First Nation but became a member of the Gambler First Nation after her marriage. Her husband passed away four years after marriage. In 2012, the complainant was nominated to run for Chief but was told that she did not qualify to run for elected office because she was

---

181 "On-Reserve Housing and Infrastructure: Recommendations for Change", The Standing Senate Committee on Aboriginal Peoples, last updated June 12, 2015, https://sencanada.ca/content/sen/committee/412/appa/rms/12jun15/Home-e.htm

182 "Annual Report of the Office of the Correctional Investigator", The Correctional Investigator Canada, last updated June 30, 2016, https://www.oci-bec.gc.ca/cnt/rpt/pdf/annrpt/annrpt20152016-eng.pdf

183 2015 CHRT 19 (CanLII)

not a blood descendant of John Falcon Tanner,[184] a signatory to Treaty 4.

The Tribunal found that such descent rule was not rationally connected to the function of being Chief or Councillor of the Gambler First Nation and, therefore, cannot be bona fide justified. The Tribunal held that the Gambler First Nation has discriminated against the complainant on the basis of race, national or ethnic origin, or family status, pursuant to section 5 of the Canadian Human Rights Act.

It is possible that all types of discrimination started with racial discrimination, and racial discrimination started with discriminating against Indigenous people. To fight discrimination, we should first fight discrimination against Indigenous people.

---

[184] "John Tanner (captive)", Wikipedia, , last accessed October 13, 2023, https://en.wikipedia.org/wiki/John_Tanner_(captive)

~ The End ~

I. Glossary of Human Rights Terms

Ableism. Ableism is the discrimination and social prejudice against people with disabilities or perceived to have disabilities. Ableism can be conscious or unconscious and is embedded in communities, institutions, systems, or society's broader culture.

Aboriginal Peoples. See Indigenous Peoples

Accessibility. It is a general term for the degree of ease with which something (e.g., building, device, service, and information) can be accessed, used and enjoyed by persons with disabilities. Easy accessibility benefits the general population, such as seniors and families with small children, by making things more usable and practical for everyone.

Accessible. It means no obstacles for people with disabilities — something that can be easily reached or obtained, facilities that can be easily entered, and information that is easy to retrieve.

Adaptive Technologies. The technologies used in some products help people with vision, hearing, mobility or other disabilities to use the products.

Adverse Impact. A harmful result, usually referring to treating people with and without disabilities, will have a negative effect on some people.

Affirmative Action. An action designed to address the historical disadvantage that identifiable groups (e.g., women and visible minorities) have experienced by increasing their representation in employment, higher education or treatment.

African Canadian. A Canadian of African origin or descent.

Ageism. Stereotypes against individuals or groups based on their age, generally with discrimination.

Ally. A member of the dominant group who is against oppression.

Alternative (Alternate) Format. A method of communication that considers the disability of a person, such as an audiobook instead of a print version for someone with a visual disability.

Anti-racism (Anti-oppression). An active and consistent process of change to eliminate racism and the oppression and injustice racism causes.

Assistive device. Devices to help people, primarily people with disabilities, perform tasks, such as assistive listening devices, forklifts and wheelchairs.

Audism. A belief that a person is superior or inferior based on their ability to hear or act like a person who hears.

Band. In Canada, the *Indian Act* defines a band as a body of Indians for whose use and benefit in common, lands have been set aside, or monies are held by the Government of Canada or declared by the Governor in Council for the purposes of the Act. Band members generally share common values, traditions and practices rooted in their ancestral heritage.

Band Council. The governing body of a band in Canada. It usually has a Chief and some Councillors elected for two or three-year terms (under the *Indian Act* or band custom) to carry out band business. That may include education, water, sewer, fire services, bylaws, community buildings, schools, roads and other community businesses and services.

Barrier. Anything that prevents a person from fully taking part in all aspects of society, including physical, information or communications, attitudinal, economic and technological barriers, as well as policies or practices.

BFOR. Acronym for Bona Fide Occupational Requirement, a defence used in discrimination in employment.

Bias. A predisposition, prejudice or generalization about a group of persons based on characteristics or stereotypes.

Bigotry. Obstinate or unreasonable attachment to a belief, opinion, or prejudice against a person or people based on stereotypes related to age, race, religion, sexual orientation, and more.

Biological Sex. The biological classification of people as male or female. Sex terms are "male", "female", and "intersex". A doctor assigns sex at birth, by visually assessing external anatomy.

Biracial. A person whose ancestry includes members of two racial groups.

Bisexual. a person who is emotionally, physically, sexually or spiritually attracted to members of more than one gender.

Black. It is a social construct referring to people with dark skin colour or other racialized characteristics. Diverse societies apply different criteria to determine who is Black.

Caste System. A form of social stratification with roots in India's ancient history and persisting to the present time. This system divides people into four classes: Brahmin, Kshatriya, Vaishya, and Shudra. In addition to the four major castes, another type of people called Dalit or untouchable is excluded from the castes.

Caucasian. An outdated term that often has been used as a synonym for white.

Characteristics. A personal trait or attribute.

Civil Union. A legally recognized arrangement similar to a marriage, created primarily to provide legal recognition for same-sex couples.

Code. It refers to the human rights code of the local jurisdiction.

Coming Out. The often life-long process of discovering, defining and proclaiming one's sexuality (usually non-heterosexual).

Competing Rights. Situations where parties to a dispute claim that the enjoyment of an individual or group's human rights and freedoms, as protected by law, would interfere with another's rights and freedoms.

Culture. The achievements, behaviours, beliefs or customs of a particular time or people; behaviour within a particular group.

Cultural Competence. An ability to interact effectively with people of different cultural or ethnic backgrounds.

Culturally Competent Organization. An organization displays cultural competence in its systems and individual behaviour.

Custom. A traditional practice.

Dimensions of Diversity. The unique personal characteristics distinguish people as individuals and groups. These include but are not limited to age, gender, race, sex, ethnicity, physical and intellectual ability, class, creed, religion and sexual orientation.

Disability. A disability may have been present from birth, caused by accident, or developed over time. It covers a broad range and degree of conditions, some visible and some not visible.

Discrimination. Discrimination occurs when an individual is mistreated through the imposition of burdens or the denial of benefits, privileges, or opportunities others enjoy based on characteristics such as age, religion, family status, disability, sex, and race.

Duty to Accommodate. The obligation to ensure people identified by human rights law are entitled to the same opportunities and benefits as everybody else.

East Asian People. People who share ancestry, heritage and culture from several countries and regions, including Mainland China, Taiwan, Hong Kong, Macau, Japan, Mongolia, North Korea, South Korea and Vietnam.

EDI. Acronym of Equity, Diversity and Inclusion.

Elder. A distinguished person recognized in the Aboriginal community for the gift of healing, spiritual or wisdom leadership.

Equal Opportunity. The concept of equal opportunity aims to ensure that all individuals have equal access, free from barriers, equal participation, and equal benefit from whatever an organization offers.

Equal Treatment. The treatment brings about equality of access, such as providing a ramp for wheelchair access to a building in addition to a stair.

Equitable. It refers to being just or characterized by fairness and equity.

Equity. It refers to the quality of fairness, impartiality, and even-handedness.

Ethnicity. It refers to the cultural and social characteristics that distinguish one group of people from another based on factors such as a distinctive cultural and historical tradition associated with ancestry, creed, place of origin or race.

Exclusion. The action of denying or limiting access to a place, group, privilege, and more.

First Nations. The term was commonly used in the 1970s to replace the word "Indian", the predominant Indigenous peoples in Canada south of the Arctic Circle.

Francophone. People with advanced knowledge of French use it at home, including those whose mother tongue may not be French.

Gay. Persons have an emotional, physical, sexual or spiritual attraction to persons of the same sex.

Gender. The social classification of people as masculine or feminine.

Gender Identity. The conscious sense of maleness or femaleness of a person. This sense of self is separate and distinct from one's biological sex.

Harassment. It involves making comments or engaging in actions that are known or should reasonably be known as unwelcome. It can include words or actions known (or ought reasonably to be known) to be demeaning, embarrassing, humiliating, offensive, or unwelcome.

Hate Activity. It involves negative comments or unfriendly actions against a person or group motivated by bias, prejudice or hate based on, including but not limited to, age, ancestry, race, ethnic origin, language, colour, religion, mental disability, physical disability, family status, marital status, sex, and sexual orientation.

Heightism. The prejudice or discrimination against individuals based on height.

Heterosexual. Persons have an emotional, physical, sexual or spiritual attraction to persons of the opposite sex.

Heterosexism. A belief that heterosexuality is superior and preferable to other sexualities and that heterosexuality is the only right, normal or moral expression of sexuality.

Historical Disadvantage. The disadvantage arises from historical patterns of institutionalized discrimination and other systemic forms.

Homosexual. An outdated term for persons with an emotional, physical, sexual or spiritual attraction to persons of the same sex. It is more of a medical term and may insult lesbian and gay people or the LGBT community.

Homophobia. The irrational aversion to, fear or hatred of people identified or perceived as lesbian, gay, bisexual or transgender (LGBT).

Impairment. A physical, sensory, intellectual, learning or medical condition, including mental illness, that limits functioning or requires accommodation.

Inclusion. Inclusion involves recognizing and utilizing our distinct differences, encompassing strengths, talents, weaknesses, and vulnerabilities, to demonstrate respect for each individual and foster the development of a vibrant and diverse community.

Inclusive Design. It encompasses applying inclusive design principles to systems, facilities, programs, policies, services, education, and other aspects. It involves considering the variations among individuals and groups when creating something to prevent the creation of barriers.

Indian. This term is used to identify people the Government of Canada recognizes as having Indian status — people who have an identifiable band, live or were born on a reserve, or are recognized under a complex set of rules under the *Indian Act (1985*). The term does not include Inuit or Métis peoples. There are three categories of Indians in Canada: Status Indians, Non-Status Indians, and Treaty Indians. It is considered outdated by many people, and First Nations is typically used instead.

Indian Act. A Canadian act passed in 1876 and was amended several times since, most recently in 2019. It sets out certain federal government obligations and regulates the management of reserve lands, Indian monies and other resources.

Indian Status. A person's legal status as an "Indian" is defined under the *Indian Act* of Canada.

Indigenous Peoples. Also known as Aboriginal Peoples. A collective name for the native people of North America and their descendants. The Canadian Constitution (the *Constitution Act,* 1982) recognizes three groups of Indigenous Peoples — First Nations, Métis and Inuit — as separate peoples with unique heritages, languages, cultural practices and spiritual beliefs.

Intellectual Disability. Also called a developmental disability, it involves significant limitations in intellectual functioning (reasoning, learning, problem-solving) and adaptive behaviour, which covers a range of everyday social and practical skills.

Intergenerational. Existing or occurring between different generations of people, involving more than one generation.

Intersex. A term used for a variety of conditions in which a person is born with genitalia that does not seem to fit the typical definitions of female or male, formerly inappropriately referred to as hermaphrodites. Most intersex people do not possess "both" sets of genitals but rather a blending or a different appearance that is medically difficult to categorize for many doctors.

Inuit. A group of culturally similar Indigenous peoples inhabiting the Arctic regions of Canada live primarily in Nunavut, Northwest Territories, Yukon and northern parts of Labrador and Québec. The word Inuit means "people" in the Inuit language — Inuktitut. The singular of Inuit is Inuk. Their traditional languages, customs and cultures are distinctly different from those of the First Nations and Métis.

Lesbian. A woman who has an emotional, physical, sexual or spiritual attraction to other women.

LGBT. An acronym for Lesbian, Gay, Bisexual and Transgender. Sometimes, GLBT is also used.

LGBTTIQQ2A. An acronym for Lesbian, Gay, Bisexual, Transgender, Transsexual, Intersex, Queer, Questioning, 2-spirited and Allies.

Merit. Pick a candidate who meets job-related selection criteria, such as experience, knowledge and skills, at the level required for a position or assignment.

Métis. A multi-ancestral Indigenous group in Canada, a French term meaning "mixed blood". This term is used broadly to describe people with mixed First Nations and European ancestry who identify themselves as Métis, distinct from First Nations people, Inuit or non-Aboriginal people. It is one of the three Aboriginal Peoples recognized by the Canadian Constitution.

MSM. An acronym for Men who have Sex with Men.

Multiracial. A person whose heritage includes members of multiple racial groups.

Native Groups. Indigenous people in the United States.

Pay Equity. The principle of equal pay for work of equal value. For example, the principle is applied to pay male and female employees within the same organization the same salary for work that is judged to be of equal value.

Persons of Colour. An inclusive term encompassing a range of social identity groups based on their skin colour, such as Asians, Aboriginal Peoples, Hispanics and Blacks.

Persons with Disabilities. Persons with one or more long-term or recurring disabilities.

Poisoned Work Environment. A negative, hostile or unpleasant workplace due to comments or conduct that tends to demean a group identified by one or more prohibited grounds under any Human Rights Act or Code, even if not directed at a specific individual.

Power. Access to privileges such as connections, decision-making, experience, expertise, resources, knowledge and information that enhance a person's chances of getting what they need to live a comfortable, safe, productive and profitable life.

Prejudice. Affective feeling or negative prejudgment about another person or group of persons based on perceived characteristics.

Pride. A term used about the LGBT community. It means people not being ashamed of themselves or showing their pride to others by "coming out", marching in the Pride parade or similar parades, and being honest and comfortable about who they are.

Pride Parade. An outdoor event that celebrates LGBT achievements, legal rights, pride, self and social acceptance

Privilege. Unearned access, advantages, benefits, opportunities or power that exist for members of the dominant groups in society. It can also refer to the relative privilege of one group compared to another.

Prohibited Grounds (Protected Grounds). The personal characteristics that the human rights law is based on to prohibit discrimination or harassment. The common protected grounds include age, ancestry, citizenship, colour, creed, disability, ethnic origin, family status, gender identity and gender expression, marital status, place of origin, race, receipt of public assistance (in housing), a record of offences (in employment), sex and sexual orientation.

Queer. Formerly derogatory slang term used to identify sexual and gender minorities who are not heterosexual.

Questioning. Exploring one's own sexual or gender identity, looking at such things as upbringing, expectations from others, such as friends and employers, and inner motivation.

Race. A group of people with similar geographic, historical, political, economic, physical, social, and cultural factors.

Racialization. The process by which societies construct races as real, different and unequal in ways that matter and affect economic, political and social life.

Racial Profiling. Any action that relies on stereotypes about race, ancestry, colour, ethnicity, religion, place of origin, or a combination of these rather than on a reasonable suspicion to single out a person for greater scrutiny or different treatment.

Racism. A belief that one race group is superior or inferior to others.

Sexism. A belief that one gender type is superior or inferior to another. It is usually linked with discrimination.

Sexual Orientation. The direction of one's sexual interest or attraction. It covers the range of human sexuality from lesbian and gay to bisexual and heterosexual.

South Asian. A native or inhabitant of the Indian subcontinent, including Afghanistan, Bangladesh, Bhutan, India, the Maldives, Nepal, Pakistan, and Sri Lanka.

Status Indian. A person recognized by the federal government as being registered under the *Indian Act.* It is also referred to as a Registered Indian.

Stereotype. Incorrect assumptions based on age, sex, race, colour, ethnic origin, religion, and more. Stereotyping typically involves attributing the same characteristics to all members of a group regardless of their differences.

Straight. An informal term for Heterosexual.

Systemic Barrier. The barrier may exclude members of groups protected by human rights laws. It is embedded in the administrative or social structures of an organization, including the culture, decision-making processes, physical accessibility, policies and practices of an organization.

Systemic Discrimination. Patterns of behaviour, policies or practices that are part of the social or administrative structures of an organization and which create or perpetuate a position of relative disadvantage for groups identified under the human rights law.

Two-Spirit. A term that refers to Aboriginal people who are gay, lesbian, bisexual, or trans-gendered.

Transgender (or Trans). A person whose biological sex assigned at birth does not match their gender identity.

Transsexual. Persons who are identified at birth as one sex but who identify themselves differently and have undergone one or more medical treatments to align their bodies with their internally felt identity. While some people embrace this term as an identity, it is rejected by others.

West Indian. A person from the West Indies, including Antigua and Barbuda, Bahamas, Barbados, Cuba, Dominica, Dominican Republic, Grenada, Haiti, Jamaica, Saint Kitts and Nevis, Saint Lucia, Saint Vincent and the Grenadines, Trinidad and Tobago.

White. People belonging to any of various peoples with light-coloured skin, usually of European origin. The term has become an indicator less of skin colour and more of racialized characteristics.

II. Canadian Human Rights Act

Canadian Human Rights Act[185]

R.S.C., 1985, c. H-6

An Act to extend the laws in Canada that proscribe discrimination

Short Title

1 This Act may be cited as the *Canadian Human Rights Act.*

1976-77, c. 33, s. 1

Purpose of Act

2 The purpose of this Act is to extend the laws in Canada to give effect, within the purview of matters coming within the legislative authority of Parliament, to the principle that all individuals should have an opportunity equal with other individuals to make for themselves the lives that they are able and wish to have and to have their needs accommodated, consistent with their duties and obligations as members of society, without being hindered in or prevented from doing so by discriminatory practices based on race, national or ethnic origin, colour, religion, age, sex, sexual orientation, gender identity or expression, marital status, family status, genetic characteristics, disability or conviction for an offence for which a pardon has been granted or in respect of which a record suspension has been ordered.

R.S., 1985, c. H-6, s. 2; 1996, c. 14, s. 1; 1998, c. 9, s. 9; 2012, c. 1, s. 137(E); 2017, c. 3, ss. 9, 11, c. 13, s. 1

PART I

[185] "Canadian Human Rights Act (R.S.C., 1985, c. H-6)", Government of Canada, last accessed November 4, 2020, https://laws-lois.justice.gc.ca/eng/acts/h-6/

Proscribed Discrimination

General

Prohibited grounds of discrimination

3 (1) For all purposes of this Act, the prohibited grounds of discrimination are race, national or ethnic origin, colour, religion, age, sex, sexual orientation, gender identity or expression, marital status, family status, genetic characteristics, disability and conviction for an offence for which a pardon has been granted or in respect of which a record suspension has been ordered.

Idem

(2) Where the ground of discrimination is pregnancy or child-birth, the discrimination shall be deemed to be on the ground of sex.

Idem

(3) Where the ground of discrimination is refusal of a request to undergo a genetic test or to disclose, or authorize the disclosure of, the results of a genetic test, the discrimination shall be deemed to be on the ground of genetic characteristics.

R.S., 1985, c. H-6, s. 3; 1996, c. 14, s. 2; 2012, c. 1, s. 138(E); 2017, c. 3, ss. 10, 11, c. 13, s. 2

Multiple grounds of discrimination

3.1 For greater certainty, a discriminatory practice includes a practice based on one or more prohibited grounds of discrimination or on the effect of a combination of prohibited grounds.

1998, c. 9, s. 11

Orders regarding discriminatory practices

4 A discriminatory practice, as described in sections 5 to 14.1, may be the subject of a complaint under Part III and anyone found to be engaging or to have engaged in a discriminatory practice may be made subject to an order as provided in section 53.

R.S., 1985, c. H-6, s. 4; 1998, c. 9, s. 11; 2013, c. 37, s. 1

Discriminatory Practices

Denial of good, service, facility or accommodation

5 It is a discriminatory practice in the provision of goods, services, facilities or accommodation customarily available to the general public

(a) to deny, or to deny access to, any such good, service, facility or accommodation to any individual, or

(b) to differentiate adversely in relation to any individual,

on a prohibited ground of discrimination.

1976-77, c. 33, s. 5

Denial of commercial premises or residential accommodation

6 It is a discriminatory practice in the provision of commercial premises or residential accommodation

(a) to deny occupancy of such premises or accommodation to any individual, or

(b) to differentiate adversely in relation to any individual,

on a prohibited ground of discrimination.

1976-77, c. 33, s. 6

Employment

7 It is a discriminatory practice, directly or indirectly,

(a) to refuse to employ or continue to employ any individual, or

(b) in the course of employment, to differentiate adversely in relation to an employee,

on a prohibited ground of discrimination.

1976-77, c. 33, s. 7; 1980-81-82-83, c. 143, s. 3(F)

Employment applications, advertisements

8 It is a discriminatory practice

(a) to use or circulate any form of application for employment, or

(b) in connection with employment or prospective employment, to publish any advertisement or to make any written or oral inquiry

that expresses or implies any limitation, specification or preference based on a prohibited ground of discrimination.

1976-77, c. 33, s. 8

Employee organizations

9 (1) It is a discriminatory practice for an employee organization on a prohibited ground of discrimination

(a) to exclude an individual from full membership in the organization;

(b) to expel or suspend a member of the organization; or

(c) to limit, segregate, classify or otherwise act in relation to an individual in a way that would deprive the individual of employment opportunities, or limit employment opportunities or otherwise adversely affect the status of the individual, where the individual is a member of the organization or where any of the obligations of the organization pursuant to a collective agreement relate to the individual.

(2) [Repealed, 2011, c. 24, s. 165]

(3) [Repealed, 1998, c. 9, s. 12]

R.S., 1985, c. H-6, s. 9; 1998, c. 9, s. 12; 2011, c. 24, s. 165

Discriminatory policy or practice

10 It is a discriminatory practice for an employer, employee organization or employer organization

(a) to establish or pursue a policy or practice, or

(b) to enter into an agreement affecting recruitment, referral, hiring, promotion, training, apprenticeship, transfer or any other matter relating to employment or prospective employment,

that deprives or tends to deprive an individual or class of individuals of any employment opportunities on a prohibited ground of discrimination.

R.S., 1985, c. H-6, s. 10; 1998, c. 9, s. 13(E)

Equal wages

11 (1) It is a discriminatory practice for an employer to establish or maintain differences in wages between male and female employees employed in the same establishment who are performing work of equal value.

Assessment of value of work

(2) In assessing the value of work performed by employees employed in the same establishment, the criterion to be applied is the composite of the skill, effort and responsibility required in the performance of the work and the conditions under which the work is performed.

Separate establishments

(3) Separate establishments established or maintained by an employer solely or principally for the purpose of establishing or maintaining differences in wages between male and female employees shall be deemed for the purposes of this section to be the same establishment.

Different wages based on prescribed reasonable factors

(4) Notwithstanding subsection (1), it is not a discriminatory practice to pay to male and female employees different wages if the difference is based on a factor prescribed by guidelines, issued by the Canadian Human Rights Commission pursuant to subsection 27(2), to be a reasonable factor that justifies the difference.

Idem

(5) For greater certainty, sex does not constitute a reasonable factor justifying a difference in wages.

No reduction of wages

(6) An employer shall not reduce wages in order to eliminate a discriminatory practice described in this section.

Definition of wages

(7) For the purposes of this section, wages means any form of remuneration payable for work performed by an individual and includes

(a) salaries, commissions, vacation pay, dismissal wages and bonuses;

(b) reasonable value for board, rent, housing and lodging;

(c) payments in kind;

(d) employer contributions to pension funds or plans, long-term disability plans and all forms of health insurance plans; and

(e) any other advantage received directly or indirectly from the individual's employer.

1976-77, c. 33, s. 11

Publication of discriminatory notices, etc.

12 It is a discriminatory practice to publish or display before the public or to cause to be published or displayed before the public any notice, sign, symbol, emblem or other representation that

(a) expresses or implies discrimination or an intention to discriminate, or

(b) incites or is calculated to incite others to discriminate

if the discrimination expressed or implied, intended to be expressed or implied or incited or calculated to be incited would otherwise, if engaged in, be a discriminatory practice described in any of sections 5 to 11 or in section 14.

1976-77, c. 33, s. 12; 1980-81-82-83, c. 143, s. 6

13 [Repealed, 2013, c. 37, s. 2]

Harassment

14 (1) It is a discriminatory practice,

(a) in the provision of goods, services, facilities or accommodation customarily available to the general public,

(b) in the provision of commercial premises or residential accommodation, or

(c) in matters related to employment,

to harass an individual on a prohibited ground of discrimination.

Sexual harassment

(2) Without limiting the generality of subsection (1), sexual harassment shall, for the purposes of that subsection, be deemed to be harassment on a prohibited ground of discrimination.

1980-81-82-83, c. 143, s. 7

Retaliation

14.1 It is a discriminatory practice for a person against whom a complaint has been filed under Part III, or any person acting on their behalf, to retaliate or threaten retaliation against the individual who filed the complaint or the alleged victim.

1998, c. 9, s. 14

Exceptions

15 (1) It is not a discriminatory practice if

(a) any refusal, exclusion, expulsion, suspension, limitation, specification or preference in relation to any employment is established by an employer to be based on a *bona fide* occupational requirement;

(b) employment of an individual is refused or terminated because that individual has not reached the minimum age, or has reached the maximum age, that applies to that employment by law or under regulations, which may be made by the Governor in Council for the purposes of this paragraph;

(c) [Repealed, 2011, c. 24, s. 166]

(d) the terms and conditions of any pension fund or plan established by an employer, employee organization or employer organization provide for the compulsory vesting or locking-in of pension contributions at a fixed or determinable age in accordance with sections 17 and 18 of the *Pension Benefits Standards Act, 1985*;

(d.1) the terms of any pooled registered pension plan provide for variable payments or the transfer of funds only at a fixed age under sections 48 or 55, respectively, of the *Pooled Registered Pension Plans Act*;

(e) an individual is discriminated against on a prohibited ground of discrimination in a manner that is prescribed by guidelines, issued by the Canadian Human Rights Commission pursuant to subsection 27(2), to be reasonable;

(f) an employer, employee organization or employer organization grants a female employee special leave or benefits in connection with pregnancy or child-birth or grants employees special leave or benefits to assist them in the care of their children; or

(g) in the circumstances described in section 5 or 6, an individual is denied any goods, services, facilities or accommodation or access thereto or occupancy of any commercial premises or residential accommodation or is a victim of any adverse differentiation and there is *bona fide* justification for that denial or differentiation.

Accommodation of needs

(2) For any practice mentioned in paragraph (1)(a) to be considered to be based on a *bona fide* occupational requirement and for any practice mentioned in paragraph (1)(g) to be considered to have a *bona fide* justification, it must be established that accommodation of the needs of an individual or a class of individuals affected would impose undue hardship on the person who would have to accommodate those needs, considering health, safety and cost.

Regulations

(3) The Governor in Council may make regulations prescribing standards for assessing undue hardship.

Publication of proposed regulations

(4) Each regulation that the Governor in Council proposes to make under subsection (3) shall be published in the *Canada Gazette* and a reasonable opportunity shall be given to interested persons to make representations in respect of it.

Consultations

(5) The Canadian Human Rights Commission shall conduct public consultations concerning any regulation proposed to be made by the Governor in Council under subsection (3) and shall file a report of the results of the consultations with the Minister within a reasonable time after the publication of the proposed regulation in the *Canada Gazette*.

Exception

(6) A proposed regulation need not be published more than once, whether or not it has been amended as a result of any representations.

Making of regulations

(7) The Governor in Council may proceed to make regulations under subsection (3) after six months have elapsed since the publication of the proposed regulations in the *Canada Gazette*, whether or not a report described in subsection (5) is filed.

Application

(8) This section applies in respect of a practice regardless of whether it results in direct discrimination or adverse effect discrimination.

Universality of service for Canadian Forces

(9) Subsection (2) is subject to the principle of universality of service under which members of the Canadian Forces must at all times and under any circumstances perform any functions that they may be required to perform.

R.S., 1985, c. H-6, s. 15; R.S., 1985, c. 32 (2nd Supp.), s. 41; 1998, c. 9, ss. 10, 15; 2011, c. 24, s. 166; 2012, c. 16, s. 83

Special programs

16 (1) It is not a discriminatory practice for a person to adopt or carry out a special program, plan or arrangement designed to prevent disadvantages that are likely to be suffered by, or to eliminate or reduce disadvantages that are suffered by, any group of individuals when those disadvantages would be based on or related to the prohibited grounds of discrimination, by improving opportunities respecting goods, services, facilities, accommodation or employment in relation to that group.

Advice and assistance

(2) The Canadian Human Rights Commission, may

(a) make general recommendations concerning desirable objectives for special programs, plans or arrangements referred to in subsection (1); and

(b) on application, give such advice and assistance with respect to the adoption or carrying out of a special program, plan or arrangement referred to in subsection (1) as will serve to aid in the achievement of the objectives the program, plan or arrangement was designed to achieve.

Collection of information relating to prohibited grounds

(3) It is not a discriminatory practice to collect information relating to a prohibited ground of discrimination if the information is intended to be used in adopting or carrying out a special program, plan or arrangement under subsection (1).

R.S., 1985, c. H-6, s. 16; 1998, c. 9, s. 16

Plans to meet the needs of disabled persons

17 (1) A person who proposes to implement a plan for adapting any services, facilities, premises, equipment or operations to meet the needs of persons arising from a disability may apply to the Canadian Human Rights Commission for approval of the plan.

Approval of plan

(2) The Commission may, by written notice to a person making an application pursuant to subsection (1), approve the plan if the Commission is satisfied that the plan is appropriate for meeting the needs of persons arising from a disability.

Effect of approval of accommodation plan

(3) Where any services, facilities, premises, equipment or operations are adapted in accordance with a plan approved under subsection (2), matters for which the plan provides do not constitute any basis for a complaint under Part III regarding discrimination based on any disability in respect of which the plan was approved.

Notice when application not granted

(4) When the Commission decides not to grant an application made pursuant to subsection (1), it shall send a written notice of its decision to the applicant setting out the reasons for its decision.

1980-81-82-83, c. 143, s. 9

Rescinding approval of plan

18 (1) If the Canadian Human Rights Commission is satisfied that, by reason of any change in circumstances, a plan approved under subsection

17(2) has ceased to be appropriate for meeting the needs of persons arising from a disability, the Commission may, by written notice to the person who proposes to carry out or maintains the adaptation contemplated by the plan or any part thereof, rescind its approval of the plan to the extent required by the change in circumstances.

Effect where approval rescinded

(2) To the extent to which approval of a plan is rescinded under subsection (1), subsection 17(3) does not apply to the plan if the discriminatory practice to which the complaint relates is subsequent to the rescission of the approval.

Statement of reasons for rescinding approval

(3) Where the Commission rescinds approval of a plan pursuant to subsection (1), it shall include in the notice referred to therein a statement of its reasons therefor.

1980-81-82-83, c. 143, s. 9

Opportunity to make representations

19 (1) Before making its decision on an application or rescinding approval of a plan pursuant to section 17 or 18, the Canadian Human Rights Commission shall afford each person directly concerned with the matter an opportunity to make representations with respect thereto.

Restriction on deeming plan inappropriate

(2) For the purposes of sections 17 and 18, a plan shall not, by reason only that it does not conform to any standards prescribed pursuant to section 24, be deemed to be inappropriate for meeting the needs of persons arising from disability.

1980-81-82-83, c. 143, s. 9

Certain provisions not discriminatory

20 A provision of a pension or insurance fund or plan that preserves rights acquired before March 1, 1978 or that preserves pension or other benefits accrued before that day does not constitute the basis for a complaint under Part III that an employer, employee organization or employer organization is engaging or has engaged in a discriminatory practice.

R.S., 1985, c. H-6, s. 20; 1998, c. 9, s. 17

Funds and plans

21 The establishment of separate pension funds or plans for different groups of employees does not constitute the basis for a complaint under Part III that an employer, employee organization or employer organization is engaging or has engaged in a discriminatory practice if the employees are not grouped in those funds or plans according to a prohibited ground of discrimination.

R.S., 1985, c. H-6, s. 21; 1998, c. 9, s. 17

Regulations

22 The Governor in Council may, by regulation, prescribe the provisions of any pension or insurance fund or plan, in addition to the provisions described in sections 20 and 21, that do not constitute the basis for a complaint under Part III that an employer, employee organization or employer organization is engaging or has engaged in a discriminatory practice.

R.S., 1985, c. H-6, s. 22; 1998, c. 9, s. 17

Regulations

23 The Governor in Council may make regulations respecting the terms and conditions to be included in or applicable to any contract, licence or grant made or granted by Her Majesty in right of Canada providing for

(a) the prohibition of discriminatory practices described in sections 5 to 14.1; and

(b) the resolution, by the procedure set out in Part III, of complaints of discriminatory practices contrary to such terms and conditions.

R.S., 1985, c. H-6, s. 23; 1998, c. 9, s. 18

Accessibility standards

24 (1) The Governor in Council may, for the benefit of persons having any disability, make regulations prescribing standards of accessibility to services, facilities or premises.

Effect of meeting accessibility standards

(2) Where standards prescribed pursuant to subsection (1) are met in providing access to any services, facilities or premises, a matter of access thereto does not constitute any basis for a complaint under Part III regarding discrimination based on any disability in respect of which the standards are prescribed.

Publication of proposed regulations

(3) Subject to subsection (4), a copy of each regulation that the Governor in Council proposes to make pursuant to this section shall be published in the *Canada Gazette* and a reasonable opportunity shall be afforded to interested persons to make representations with respect thereto.

Exception

(4) Subsection (3) does not apply in respect of a proposed regulation that has been published pursuant to that subsection, whether or not it has been amended as a result of representations made pursuant to that subsection.

Discriminatory practice not constituted by variance from standards

(5) Nothing shall, by virtue only of its being at variance with any standards prescribed pursuant to subsection (1), be deemed to constitute a discriminatory practice.

1980-81-82-83, c. 143, s. 11

Definitions

25 In this Act,

conviction for an offence for which a pardon has been granted or in respect of which a record suspension has been ordered means a conviction of an individual for an offence in respect of which a pardon has been granted under Her Majesty's royal prerogative of mercy or under section 748 of the *Criminal Code* or a record suspension has been ordered under the *Criminal Records Act*, that has not been revoked or ceased to have effect; (*état de personne graciée*)

conviction for which a pardon has been granted [Repealed, 2012, c. 1, s. 139]

disability means any previous or existing mental or physical disability and includes disfigurement and previous or existing dependence on alcohol or a drug; (*déficience*) employee organization includes a trade union or other organization of employees or a local, the purposes of which include the negotiation of terms and conditions of employment on behalf of employees; (*organisation syndicale*)

employer organization means an organization of employers the purposes of which include the regulation of relations between employers and employees; (*organisation patronale*)

employment includes a contractual relationship with an individual for the provision of services personally by the individual; (*emploi*)

Tribunal means the Canadian Human Rights Tribunal established by section 48.1. (*Tribunal*)

R.S., 1985, c. H-6, s. 25; 1992, c. 22, s. 13; 1998, c. 9, s. 19; 2012, c. 1, s. 139

PART II

Canadian Human Rights Commission

Commission established

26 (1) A commission is established to be known as the Canadian Human Rights Commission, in this Act referred to as the "Commission", consisting of a Chief Commissioner, a Deputy Chief Commissioner, a member referred to as the "Accessibility Commissioner" and not less than three or more than six other members, to be appointed by the Governor in Council.

Members

(2) The Chief Commissioner, the Deputy Chief Commissioner and the Accessibility Commissioner are full-time members of the Commission and the other members may be appointed as full-time or part-time members of the Commission.

Term of appointment

(3) Each full-time member of the Commission may be appointed for a term not exceeding seven years and each part-time member may be appointed for a term not exceeding three years.

Tenure

(4) Each member of the Commission holds office during good behaviour but may be removed by the Governor in Council on address of the Senate and House of Commons.

Re-appointment

(5) A member of the Commission is eligible to be re-appointed in the same or another capacity.

R.S., 1985, c. H-6, s. 26; 2019, c. 10, s. 148

Powers, Duties and Functions

Powers, duties and functions

27 (1) In addition to its duties under Part III with respect to complaints regarding discriminatory practices, the Commission is generally responsible for the administration of this Part and Parts I and III and

(a) shall develop and conduct information programs to foster public understanding of this Act and of the role and activities of the Commission thereunder and to foster public recognition of the principle described in section 2;

(b) shall undertake or sponsor research programs relating to its duties and functions under this Act and respecting the principle described in section 2;

(c) shall maintain close liaison with similar bodies or authorities in the provinces in order to foster common policies and practices and to avoid conflicts respecting the handling of complaints in cases of overlapping jurisdiction;

(d) shall perform duties and functions to be performed by it pursuant to any agreement entered into under subsection 28(2);

(e) may consider such recommendations, suggestions and requests concerning human rights and freedoms as it receives from any source and, where deemed by the Commission to be appropriate, include in a report referred to in section 61 reference to and comment on any such recommendation, suggestion or request;

(f) shall carry out or cause to be carried out such studies concerning human rights and freedoms as may be referred to it by the Minister of

Justice and include in a report referred to in section 61 a report setting out the results of each such study together with such recommendations in relation thereto as it considers appropriate;

(g) may review any regulations, rules, orders, by-laws and other instruments made pursuant to an Act of Parliament and, where deemed by the Commission to be appropriate, include in a report referred to in section 61 reference to and comment on any provision thereof that in its opinion is inconsistent with the principle described in section 2; and

(h) shall, so far as is practical and consistent with the application of Part III, try by persuasion, publicity or any other means that it considers appropriate to discourage and reduce discriminatory practices referred to in sections 5 to 14.1.

Guidelines

(2) The Commission may, on application or on its own initiative, by order, issue a guideline setting out the extent to which and the manner in which, in the opinion of the Commission, any provision of this Act applies in a class of cases described in the guideline.

Guideline binding

(3) A guideline issued under subsection (2) is, until it is revoked or modified, binding on the Commission and any member or panel assigned under subsection 49(2) with respect to the resolution of a complaint under Part III regarding a case falling within the description contained in the guideline.

Publication

(4) Each guideline issued under subsection (2) shall be published in Part II of the *Canada Gazette*.

R.S., 1985, c. H-6, s. 27;1998, c. 9, s. 20

Assignment of duties

28 (1) On the recommendation of the Commission, the Governor in Council may, by order, assign to persons or classes of persons specified in the order who are engaged in the performance of the duties and functions of the Department of Employment and Social Development such of the duties and functions of the Commission in relation to

discriminatory practices in employment outside the federal public administration as are specified in the order.

Interdelegation

(2) Subject to the approval of the Governor in Council, the Commission may enter into agreements with similar bodies or authorities in the provinces providing for the performance by the Commission on behalf of those bodies or authorities of duties or functions specified in the agreements or for the performance by those bodies or authorities on behalf of the Commission of duties or functions so specified.

R.S., 1985, c. H-6, s. 28; 1996, c. 11, s. 61; 2003, c. 22, s. 224(E); 2005, c. 34, s. 79; 2013, c. 40, s. 237

Convention on the Rights of Persons with Disabilities

28.1 The Commission is, for the purposes of paragraph 2 of article 33 of the Convention on the Rights of Persons with Disabilities, adopted by the General Assembly of the United Nations on December 13, 2006, designated as a body responsible for monitoring the Government of Canada's implementation of that Convention.

2019, c. 10, s. 149

Regulations

29 The Governor in Council, on the recommendation of the Commission, may make regulations authorizing the Commission to exercise such powers and perform such duties and functions, in addition to those prescribed by this Act, as are necessary to carry out the provisions of this Part and Parts I and III.

1976-77, c. 33, s. 23

Remuneration

Salaries and remuneration

30 (1) Each full-time member of the Commission shall be paid a salary to be fixed by the Governor in Council and each part-time member of the Commission may be paid such remuneration, as is prescribed by by-law of the Commission, for attendance at meetings of the Commission, or of

any division or committee of the Commission, that the member is requested by the Chief Commissioner to attend.

Additional remuneration

(2) A part-time member of the Commission may, for any period during which that member, with the approval of the Chief Commissioner, performs any duties and functions additional to the normal duties and functions of that member on behalf of the Commission, be paid such additional remuneration as is prescribed by by-law of the Commission.

Travel expenses

(3) Each member of the Commission is entitled to be paid such travel and living expenses incurred by the member in the performance of duties and functions under this Act as are prescribed by by-law of the Commission.

1976-77, c. 33, s. 24

Officers and Staff

Chief Commissioner

31 (1) The Chief Commissioner is the chief executive officer of the Commission and has supervision over and direction of the Commission and its staff and shall preside at meetings of the Commission.

Absence or incapacity

(2) In the event of the absence or incapacity of the Chief Commissioner, or if that office is vacant, the Deputy Chief Commissioner has all the powers and may perform all the duties and functions of the Chief Commissioner.

Absence or incapacity of Chief and Deputy Chief

(3) In the event of the absence or incapacity of the Chief Commissioner and the Deputy Chief Commissioner, or if those offices are vacant, the full-time member, other than the Accessibility Commissioner, with the most seniority has all the powers and may perform all the duties and functions of the Chief Commissioner.

R.S., 1985, c. H-6, s. 31; 2019, c. 10, s. 150

Staff

32 (1) Such officers and employees as are necessary for the proper conduct of the work of the Commission shall be appointed in accordance with the *Public Service Employment Act*.

Contractual assistance

(2) The Commission may, for specific projects, enter into contracts for the services of persons having technical or specialized knowledge of any matter relating to the work of the Commission to advise and assist the Commission in the exercise of its powers or the performance of its duties and functions under this Act, and those persons may be paid such remuneration and expenses as may be prescribed by by-law of the Commission.

1976-77, c. 33, s. 26

Accessibility unit

32.1 The officers and employees of the Commission that support the Accessibility Commissioner in the exercise of his or her powers and the performance of his or her duties and functions under the *Accessible Canada Act* may be referred to as the "Accessibility Unit".

2019, c. 10, s. 151

Compliance with security requirements

33 (1) Every member of the Commission and every person employed by the Commission who is required to receive or obtain information relating to any investigation under this Act shall, with respect to access to and the use of such information, comply with any security requirements applicable to, and take any oath of secrecy required to be taken by, individuals who normally have access to and use of such information.

Disclosure

(2) Every member of the Commission and every person employed by the Commission shall take every reasonable precaution to avoid disclosing any matter the disclosure of which

(a) might be injurious to international relations, national defence or security or federal-provincial relations;

(b) would disclose a confidence of the Queen's Privy Council for Canada;

(c) would be likely to disclose information obtained or prepared by any investigative body of the Government of Canada

(i) in relation to national security,

(ii) in the course of investigations pertaining to the detection or suppression of crime generally, or

(iii) in the course of investigations pertaining to particular offences against any Act of Parliament;

(d) might, in respect of any individual under sentence for an offence against any Act of Parliament,

(i) lead to a serious disruption of that individual's institutional, parole or mandatory supervision program,

(ii) reveal information originally obtained on a promise of confidentiality, express or implied, or

(iii) result in physical or other harm to that individual or any other person;

(e) might impede the functioning of a court of law, or a quasi-judicial board, commission or other tribunal or any inquiry established under the *Inquiries Act*; or

(f) might disclose legal opinions or advice provided to a government department or body or privileged communications between lawyer and client in a matter of government business.

1976-77, c. 33, s. 27

Head office

34 (1) The head office of the Commission shall be in the National Capital Region described in the schedule to the *National Capital Act*.

Other offices

(2) The Commission may establish such regional or branch offices, not exceeding twelve, as it considers necessary to carry out its powers, duties and functions under this Act.

Meetings

(3) The Commission may meet for the conduct of its affairs at such times and in such places as the Chief Commissioner considers necessary or desirable.

1976-77, c. 33, s. 28

Majority is a decision of the Commission

35 A decision of the majority of the members present at a meeting of the Commission, if the members present constitute a quorum, is a decision of the Commission.

1976-77, c. 33, s. 28

Establishment of divisions

36 (1) For the purposes of the affairs of the Commission, the Chief Commissioner may establish divisions of the Commission and all or any of the powers, duties and functions of the Commission, except the making of by-laws, may, as directed by the Commission, be exercised or performed by all or any of those divisions.

Designation of presiding officer

(2) Where a division of the Commission has been established pursuant to subsection (1), the Chief Commissioner may designate one of the members of the division to act as the presiding officer of the division.

1976-77, c. 33, s. 28

By-laws

37 (1) The Commission may make by-laws for the conduct of its affairs and, without limiting the generality of the foregoing, may make by-laws

(a) respecting the calling of meetings of the Commission or any division thereof and the fixing of quorums for the purposes of those meetings;

(b) respecting the conduct of business at meetings of the Commission or any division thereof;

(c) respecting the establishment of committees of the Commission, the delegation of powers, duties and functions to those committees and the fixing of quorums for meetings thereof;

(d) respecting the procedure to be followed in dealing with complaints under Part III that have arisen in Yukon, the Northwest Territories or Nunavut;

(e) prescribing the rates of remuneration to be paid to part-time members of the Commission and any person engaged under subsection 32(2); and

(f) prescribing reasonable rates of travel and living expenses to be paid to members of the Commission and any person engaged under subsection 32(2).

Treasury Board approval

(2) No by-law made under paragraph (1)(e) or (f) has effect unless it is approved by the Treasury Board.

R.S., 1985, c. H-6, s. 37; 1993, c. 28, s. 78; 1998, c. 9, s. 21; 2002, c. 7, s. 126

Superannuation, etc.

38 The full-time members of the Commission are deemed to be persons employed in the public service for the purposes of the *Public Service Superannuation Act* and to be employed in the federal public administration for the purposes of the *Government Employees Compensation Act* and any regulations made under section 9 of the *Aeronautics Act*.

R.S., 1985, c. H-6, s. 38; 2003, c. 22, s. 137(E)

Accessibility Commissioner

Powers, duties and functions

38.1 In addition to being a member of the Commission, the Accessibility Commissioner has the powers, duties and functions assigned to him or her by the *Accessible Canada Act*.

2019, c. 10, s. 152

Absence or incapacity of Accessibility Commissioner

38.2 In the event of the absence or incapacity of the Accessibility Commissioner, or if the office of Accessibility Commissioner is vacant, the Chief Commissioner may authorize any member of the Commission, other than himself or herself, to exercise the powers and perform the duties and functions of the Accessibility Commissioner, but no member may be so authorized for a term of more than 90 days without the Governor in Council's approval.

2019, c. 10, s. 152

PART III

Discriminatory Practices and General Provisions

Definition of discriminatory practice

39 For the purposes of this Part, a discriminatory practice means any practice that is a discriminatory practice within the meaning of sections 5 to 14.1.

R.S., 1985, c. H-6, s. 39; 1998, c. 9, s. 22

Complaints

40 (1) Subject to subsections (5) and (7), any individual or group of individuals having reasonable grounds for believing that a person is engaging or has engaged in a discriminatory practice may file with the Commission a complaint in a form acceptable to the Commission.

Consent of victim

(2) If a complaint is made by someone other than the individual who is alleged to be the victim of the discriminatory practice to which the complaint relates, the Commission may refuse to deal with the complaint unless the alleged victim consents thereto.

Investigation commenced by Commission

(3) Where the Commission has reasonable grounds for believing that a person is engaging or has engaged in a discriminatory practice, the Commission may initiate a complaint.

Limitation

(3.1) No complaint may be initiated under subsection (3) as a result of information obtained by the Commission in the course of the administration of the *Employment Equity Act*.

Complaints may be dealt with together

(4) If complaints are filed jointly or separately by more than one individual or group alleging that a particular person is engaging or has engaged in a discriminatory practice or a series of similar discriminatory practices and the Commission is satisfied that the complaints involve substantially the same issues of fact and law, it may deal with the complaints together under this Part and may request the Chairperson of the Tribunal to institute a single inquiry into the complaints under section 49.

No complaints to be considered in certain cases

(5) No complaint in relation to a discriminatory practice may be dealt with by the Commission under this Part unless the act or omission that constitutes the practice

(a) occurred in Canada and the victim of the practice was at the time of the act or omission either lawfully present in Canada or, if temporarily absent from Canada, entitled to return to Canada;

(b) occurred in Canada and was a discriminatory practice within the meaning of section 5, 8, 10 or 12 in respect of which no particular individual is identifiable as the victim;

(c) occurred outside Canada and the victim of the practice was at the time of the act or omission a Canadian citizen or an individual lawfully admitted to Canada for permanent residence.

Determination of status

(6) Where a question arises under subsection (5) as to the status of an individual in relation to a complaint, the Commission shall refer the question of status to the appropriate Minister and shall not proceed with the complaint unless the question of status is resolved thereby in favour of the complainant.

No complaints to be dealt with in certain cases

(7) No complaint may be dealt with by the Commission pursuant to subsection (1) that relates to the terms and conditions of a

superannuation or pension fund or plan, if the relief sought would require action to be taken that would deprive any contributor to, participant in or member of, the fund or plan of any rights acquired under the fund or plan before March 1, 1978 or of any pension or other benefits accrued under the fund or plan to that date, including

(a) any rights and benefits based on a particular age of retirement; and

(b) any accrued survivor's benefits.

R.S., 1985, c. H-6, s. 40; R.S., 1985, c. 31 (1st Supp.), s. 62; 1995, c. 44, s. 47; 1998, c. 9, s. 23; 2013, c. 37, s. 3

Disclosure of personal information

40.01 For the purpose of the administration of the *Accessible Canada Act*, an officer or employee of the Commission may disclose to the Accessibility Commissioner any personal information that is contained in a complaint filed with the Commission.

2019, c. 10, s. 153

Definitions

40.1 (1) In this section,

designated groups has the meaning assigned in section 3 of the *Employment Equity Act*; (*groupes désignés*)

employer means a person who or organization that discharges the obligations of an employer under the *Employment Equity Act*. (*employeur*)

Employment equity complaints

(2) No complaint may be dealt with by the Commission pursuant to section 40 where

(a) the complaint is made against an employer alleging that the employer has engaged in a discriminatory practice set out in section 7 or paragraph 10(a); and

(b) the complaint is based solely on statistical information that purports to show that members of one or more designated groups are underrepresented in the employer's workforce.

1995, c. 44, s. 48

Commission to deal with complaint

41 (1) Subject to section 40, the Commission shall deal with any complaint filed with it unless in respect of that complaint it appears to the Commission that

(a) the alleged victim of the discriminatory practice to which the complaint relates ought to exhaust grievance or review procedures otherwise reasonably available;

(b) the complaint is one that could more appropriately be dealt with, initially or completely, according to a procedure provided for under an Act of Parliament other than this Act;

(c) the complaint is beyond the jurisdiction of the Commission;

(d) the complaint is trivial, frivolous, vexatious or made in bad faith; or

(e) the complaint is based on acts or omissions the last of which occurred more than one year, or such longer period of time as the Commission considers appropriate in the circumstances, before receipt of the complaint.

Commission may decline to deal with complaint

(2) The Commission may decline to deal with a complaint referred to in paragraph 10(a) in respect of an employer where it is of the opinion that the matter has been adequately dealt with in the employer's employment equity plan prepared pursuant to section 10 of the *Employment Equity Act*.

Meaning of employer

(3) In this section, employer means a person who or organization that discharges the obligations of an employer under the *Employment Equity Act*.

R.S., 1985, c. H-6, s. 41; 1994, c. 26, s. 34(F); 1995, c. 44, s. 49

Notice

42 (1) Subject to subsection (2), when the Commission decides not to deal with a complaint, it shall send a written notice of its decision to the complainant setting out the reason for its decision.

Attributing fault for delay

(2) Before deciding that a complaint will not be dealt with because a procedure referred to in paragraph 41(a) has not been exhausted, the Commission shall satisfy itself that the failure to exhaust the procedure was attributable to the complainant and not to another.

1976-77, c. 33, s. 34

Investigation

Designation of investigator

43 (1) The Commission may designate a person, in this Part referred to as an "investigator", to investigate a complaint.

Manner of investigation

(2) An investigator shall investigate a complaint in a manner authorized by regulations made pursuant to subsection (4).

Power to enter

(2.1) Subject to such limitations as the Governor in Council may prescribe in the interests of national defence or security, an investigator with a warrant issued under subsection (2.2) may, at any reasonable time, enter and search any premises in order to carry out such inquiries as are reasonably necessary for the investigation of a complaint.

Authority to issue warrant

(2.2) Where on *ex parte* application a judge of the Federal Court is satisfied by information on oath that there are reasonable grounds to believe that there is in any premises any evidence relevant to the investigation of a complaint, the judge may issue a warrant under the judge's hand authorizing the investigator named therein to enter and search those premises for any such evidence subject to such conditions as may be specified in the warrant.

Use of force

(2.3) In executing a warrant issued under subsection (2.2), the investigator named therein shall not use force unless the investigator is accompanied by a peace officer and the use of force has been specifically authorized in the warrant.

Production of books

(2.4) An investigator may require any individual found in any premises entered pursuant to this section to produce for inspection or for the purpose of obtaining copies thereof or extracts therefrom any books or other documents containing any matter relevant to the investigation being conducted by the investigator.

Obstruction

(3) No person shall obstruct an investigator in the investigation of a complaint.

Regulations

(4) The Governor in Council may make regulations

(a) prescribing procedures to be followed by investigators;

(b) authorizing the manner in which complaints are to be investigated pursuant to this Part; and

(c) prescribing limitations for the purpose of subsection (2.1).

R.S., 1985, c. H-6, s. 43; R.S., 1985, c. 31 (1st Supp.), s. 63

Report

44 (1) An investigator shall, as soon as possible after the conclusion of an investigation, submit to the Commission a report of the findings of the investigation.

Action on receipt of report

(2) If, on receipt of a report referred to in subsection (1), the Commission is satisfied

(a) that the complainant ought to exhaust grievance or review procedures otherwise reasonably available, or

(b) that the complaint could more appropriately be dealt with, initially or completely, by means of a procedure provided for under an Act of Parliament other than this Act,

it shall refer the complainant to the appropriate authority.

Idem

(3) On receipt of a report referred to in subsection (1), the Commission

(a) may request the Chairperson of the Tribunal to institute an inquiry under section 49 into the complaint to which the report relates if the Commission is satisfied

(i) that, having regard to all the circumstances of the complaint, an inquiry into the complaint is warranted, and

(ii) that the complaint to which the report relates should not be referred pursuant to subsection (2) or dismissed on any ground mentioned in paragraphs 41(c) to (e); or

(b) shall dismiss the complaint to which the report relates if it is satisfied

(i) that, having regard to all the circumstances of the complaint, an inquiry into the complaint is not warranted, or

(ii) that the complaint should be dismissed on any ground mentioned in paragraphs 41(c) to (e).

Notice

(4) After receipt of a report referred to in subsection (1), the Commission

(a) shall notify in writing the complainant and the person against whom the complaint was made of its action under subsection (2) or (3); and

(b) may, in such manner as it sees fit, notify any other person whom it considers necessary to notify of its action under subsection (2) or (3).

R.S., 1985, c. H-6, s. 44; R.S., 1985, c. 31 (1st Supp.), s. 64; 1998, c. 9, s. 24

Definition of Review Agency

45 (1) In this section and section 46, Review Agency means the National Security and Intelligence Review Agency.

Complaint involving security considerations

(2) When, at any stage after the filing of a complaint and before the commencement of a hearing before a member or panel in respect of the complaint, the Commission receives written notice from a minister of the Crown that the practice to which the complaint relates was based on considerations relating to the security of Canada, the Commission may

(a) dismiss the complaint; or

(b) refer the matter to the Review Agency.

Notice

(3) After receipt of a notice mentioned in subsection (2), the Commission

(a) shall notify in writing the complainant and the person against whom the complaint was made of its action under paragraph (2)(a) or (b); and

(b) may, in such manner as it sees fit, notify any other person whom it considers necessary to notify of its action under paragraph 2(a) or (b).

Stay of procedures

(4) Where the Commission has referred the matter to the Review Agency pursuant to paragraph (2)(b), it shall not deal with the complaint until the Review Agency has, pursuant to subsection 46(1), provided it with a report in relation to the matter.

National Security and Intelligence Review Agency Act

(5) If a matter is referred to the Review Agency under paragraph (2)(b), sections 10 to 12, 20, 24 to 28 and 30 of the *National Security and Intelligence Review Agency Act* apply, with any necessary modifications, to the matter as if the referral were a complaint made under subsection 18(3) of that Act, except that a reference in any of those provisions to "deputy head" is to be read as a reference to the minister referred to in subsection (2).

Statement to be sent to person affected

(6) The Review Agency shall, as soon as practicable after a matter in relation to a complaint is referred to it pursuant to paragraph (2)(b), send to the complainant a statement summarizing such information available to it as will enable the complainant to be as fully informed as possible of the circumstances giving rise to the referral.

R.S., 1985, c. H-6, s. 45; 1998, c. 9, s. 25; 2019, c. 13, s. 33

Report

46 (1) On completion of its investigation under section 45, the Review Agency shall, not later than 90 days after the matter is referred to it under paragraph 45(2)(b), provide the Commission, the minister referred to in

subsection 45(2), the Director of the Canadian Security Intelligence Service and the complainant with a report containing the Agency's findings. On request of the Agency, the Commission may extend the time for providing a report.

Action on receipt of report

(2) After considering a report provided pursuant to subsection (1), the Commission

(a) may dismiss the complaint or, where it does not do so, shall proceed to deal with the complaint pursuant to this Part; and

(b) shall notify, in writing, the complainant and the person against whom the complaint was made of its action under paragraph (a) and may, in such manner as it sees fit, notify any other person whom it considers necessary to notify of that action.

1984, c. 21, s. 73; 2019, c. 13, s. 34

Conciliator

Appointment of conciliator

47 (1) Subject to subsection (2), the Commission may, on the filing of a complaint, or if the complaint has not been

(a) settled in the course of investigation by an investigator,

(b) referred or dismissed under subsection 44(2) or (3) or paragraph 45(2)(a) or 46(2)(a), or

(c) settled after receipt by the parties of the notice referred to in subsection 44(4),

appoint a person, in this Part referred to as a "conciliator", for the purpose of attempting to bring about a settlement of the complaint.

Eligibility

(2) A person is not eligible to act as a conciliator in respect of a complaint if that person has already acted as an investigator in respect of that complaint.

Confidentiality

(3) Any information received by a conciliator in the course of attempting to reach a settlement of a complaint is confidential and may not be disclosed except with the consent of the person who gave the information.

1976-77, c. 33, s. 37; 1980-81-82-83, c. 143, s. 17(F); 1984, c. 21, s. 74

Settlement

Referral of a settlement to Commission

48 (1) When, at any stage after the filing of a complaint and before the commencement of a hearing before a Human Rights Tribunal in respect thereof, a settlement is agreed on by the parties, the terms of the settlement shall be referred to the Commission for approval or rejection.

Certificate

(2) If the Commission approves or rejects the terms of a settlement referred to in subsection (1), it shall so certify and notify the parties.

Enforcement of settlement

(3) A settlement approved under this section may, for the purpose of enforcement, be made an order of the Federal Court on application to that Court by the Commission or a party to the settlement.

R.S., 1985, c. H-6, s. 48; 1998, c. 9, s. 26

Canadian Human Rights Tribunal

Establishment of Tribunal

48.1 (1) There is hereby established a tribunal to be known as the Canadian Human Rights Tribunal consisting, subject to subsection (6), of a maximum of fifteen members, including a Chairperson and a Vice-chairperson, as may be appointed by the Governor in Council.

Qualifications for appointment of members

(2) Persons appointed as members of the Tribunal must have experience, expertise and interest in, and sensitivity to, human rights.

Legal qualifications

(3) The Chairperson and Vice-chairperson must be members in good standing of the bar of a province or the Chambre des notaires du Québec for at least ten years and at least two of the other members of the Tribunal must be members in good standing of the bar of a province or the Chambre des notaires du Québec.

Regional representation

(4) Appointments are to be made having regard to the need for regional representation in the membership of the Tribunal.

Appointment of temporary members — incapacity

(5) If a member is absent or incapacitated, the Governor in Council may, despite subsection (1), appoint a temporary substitute member to act during the absence or incapacity.

Appointment of temporary members — workload

(6) The Governor in Council may appoint temporary members to the Tribunal for a term of not more than three years whenever, in the opinion of the Governor in Council, the workload of the Tribunal so requires.

R.S., 1985, c. 31 (1st Supp.), s. 65; 1998, c. 9, s. 27

Terms of office

48.2 (1) The Chairperson and Vice-chairperson are to be appointed to hold office during good behaviour for terms of not more than seven years, and the other members are to be appointed to hold office during good behaviour for terms of not more than five years, but the Chairperson may be removed from office by the Governor in Council for cause and the Vice-chairperson and the other members may be subject to remedial or disciplinary measures in accordance with section 48.3.

Acting after expiration of appointment

(2) A member whose appointment expires may, with the approval of the Chairperson, conclude any inquiry that the member has begun, and a person performing duties under this subsection is deemed to be a part-time member for the purposes of sections 48.3, 48.6, 50 and 52 to 58.

Reappointment

(3) The Chairperson, Vice-chairperson or any other member whose term has expired is eligible for reappointment in the same or any other capacity.

R.S., 1985, c. 31 (1st Supp.), s. 65; 1998, c. 9, s. 27

Remedial and disciplinary measures

48.3 (1) The Chairperson of the Tribunal may request the Minister of Justice to decide whether a member should be subject to remedial or disciplinary measures for any reason set out in paragraphs (13)(a) to (d).

Measures

(2) On receipt of the request, the Minister may take one or more of the following measures:

(a) obtain, in an informal and expeditious manner, any information that the Minister considers necessary;

(b) refer the matter for mediation, if the Minister is satisfied that the issues in relation to the request may be appropriately resolved by mediation;

(c) request of the Governor in Council that an inquiry be held under subsection (3); or

(d) advise the Chairperson that the Minister considers that it is not necessary to take further measures under this Act.

Appointment of inquirer

(3) On receipt of a request referred to in paragraph (2)(c), the Governor in Council may, on the recommendation of the Minister, appoint a judge of a superior court to conduct the inquiry.

Powers

(4) The judge has all the powers, rights and privileges that are vested in a superior court, including the power to

(a) issue a summons requiring any person to appear at the time and place specified in the summons in order to testify about all matters within the person's knowledge relative to the inquiry and to produce any document or thing relative to the inquiry that the person has or controls; and

(b) administer oaths and examine any person on oath.

Staff

(5) The judge may engage the services of counsel and other persons having technical or specialized knowledge to assist the judge in conducting the inquiry, and may establish the terms and conditions of their engagement and, with the approval of the Treasury Board, fix and pay their remuneration and expenses.

Inquiry in public

(6) Subject to subsections (7) and (8), an inquiry shall be conducted in public.

Confidentiality of inquiry

(7) The judge may, on application, take any appropriate measures and make any order that the judge considers necessary to ensure the confidentiality of the inquiry if, after having considered all available alternative measures, the judge is satisfied that

(a) there is a real and substantial risk that matters involving public security will be disclosed;

(b) there is a real and substantial risk to the fairness of the inquiry such that the need to prevent disclosure outweighs the societal interest that the inquiry be conducted in public; or

(c) there is a serious possibility that the life, liberty or security of a person will be endangered.

Confidentiality of application

(8) If the judge considers it appropriate, the judge may take any measures and make any order that the judge considers necessary to ensure the confidentiality of a hearing held in respect of an application under subsection (7).

Rules of evidence

(9) In conducting an inquiry, the judge is not bound by any legal or technical rules of evidence and may receive, and base a decision on, evidence presented in the proceedings that the judge considers credible or trustworthy in the circumstances of the case.

Intervenors

(10) An interested party may, with leave of the judge, intervene in an inquiry on any terms and conditions that the judge considers appropriate.

Right to be heard

(11) The member who is the subject of the inquiry shall be given reasonable notice of the subject-matter of the inquiry and of the time and place of any hearing and shall be given an opportunity, in person or by counsel, to be heard at the hearing, to cross-examine witnesses and to present evidence.

Report to Minister

(12) After an inquiry has been completed, the judge shall submit a report containing the judge's findings and recommendations, if any, to the Minister.

Recommendations

(13) The judge may, in the report, recommend that the member be suspended without pay or removed from office or that any other disciplinary measure or any remedial measure be taken if, in the judge's opinion, the member

(a) has become incapacitated from the proper execution of that office by reason of infirmity;

(b) has been guilty of misconduct;

(c) has failed in the proper execution of that office; or

(d) has been placed, by conduct or otherwise, in a position that is incompatible with the due execution of that office.

Transmission of report to Governor in Council

(14) When the Minister receives the report, the Minister shall send it to the Governor in Council who may, if the Governor in Council considers it appropriate, suspend the member without pay, remove the member from office or impose any other disciplinary measure or any remedial measure.

R.S., 1985, c. 31 (1st Supp.), s. 65; 1998, c. 9, s. 27

Status of members

48.4 (1) The Chairperson and Vice-chairperson are to be appointed as full-time members of the Tribunal, and the other members are to be appointed as either full-time or part-time members.

Functions of Chairperson

(2) The Chairperson has supervision over and direction of the work of the Tribunal, including the allocation of work among the members and the management of the Tribunal's internal affairs.

Functions of Vice-chairperson

(3) The Vice-chairperson shall assist the Chairperson and shall perform the functions of the Chairperson if the Chairperson is absent or unable to act or the office of Chairperson is vacant.

Acting Chairperson

(4) The Governor in Council may authorize a member of the Tribunal to perform the functions of the Chairperson on a temporary basis if the Chairperson and Vice-chairperson are absent or unable to act or if both of those offices are vacant.

R.S., 1985, c. 31 (1st Supp.), s. 65; 1998, c. 9, s. 27; 2014, c. 20, s. 414

Residence

48.5 The full-time members of the Tribunal shall reside in the National Capital Region, as described in the schedule to the *National Capital Act*, or within forty kilometres of that Region.

R.S., 1985, c. 31 (1st Supp.), s. 65; 1998, c. 9, s. 27

Remuneration

48.6 (1) The members of the Tribunal shall be paid such remuneration as may be fixed by the Governor in Council.

Travel expenses

(2) Members are entitled to be paid travel and living expenses incurred in carrying out duties as members of the Tribunal while absent from their place of residence, but the expenses must not exceed the maximum limits authorized by the Treasury Board directives for employees of the Government of Canada.

Deemed employment in federal public administration

(3) Members are deemed to be employed in the federal public administration for the purposes of the *Government Employees Compensation Act* and any regulations made under section 9 of the *Aeronautics Act*.

1998, c. 9, s. 27; 2003, c. 22, s. 224(E)

Head office

48.7 The head office of the Tribunal shall be in the National Capital Region, as described in the schedule to the *National Capital Act*.

1998, c. 9, s. 27

48.8 [Repealed, 2014, c. 20, s. 415]

Conduct of proceedings

48.9 (1) Proceedings before the Tribunal shall be conducted as informally and expeditiously as the requirements of natural justice and the rules of procedure allow.

Tribunal rules of procedure

(2) The Chairperson may make rules of procedure governing the practice and procedure before the Tribunal, including, but not limited to, rules governing

(a) the giving of notices to parties;

(b) the addition of parties and interested persons to the proceedings;

(c) the summoning of witnesses;

(d) the production and service of documents;

(e) discovery proceedings;

(f) pre-hearing conferences;

(g) the introduction of evidence;

(h) time limits within which hearings must be held and decisions must be made; and

(i) awards of interest.

Publication of proposed rules

(3) Subject to subsection (4), a copy of each rule that the Tribunal proposes to make shall be published in the *Canada Gazette* and a reasonable opportunity shall be given to interested persons to make representations with respect to it.

Exception

(4) A proposed rule need not be published more than once, whether or not it has been amended as a result of any representations.

1998, c. 9, s. 27

Inquiries into Complaints

Request for inquiry

49 (1) At any stage after the filing of a complaint, the Commission may request the Chairperson of the Tribunal to institute an inquiry into the complaint if the Commission is satisfied that, having regard to all the circumstances of the complaint, an inquiry is warranted.

Chairperson to institute inquiry

(2) On receipt of a request, the Chairperson shall institute an inquiry by assigning a member of the Tribunal to inquire into the complaint, but the Chairperson may assign a panel of three members if he or she considers that the complexity of the complaint requires the inquiry to be conducted by three members.

Chair of panel

(3) If a panel of three members has been assigned to inquire into the complaint, the Chairperson shall designate one of them to chair the inquiry, but the Chairperson shall chair the inquiry if he or she is a member of the panel.

Copy of rules to parties

(4) The Chairperson shall make a copy of the rules of procedure available to each party to the complaint.

Qualification of member

(5) If the complaint involves a question about whether another Act or a regulation made under another Act is inconsistent with this Act or a regulation made under it, the member assigned to inquire into the complaint or, if three members have been assigned, the member chairing the inquiry, must be a member of the bar of a province or the Chambre des notaires du Québec.

Question raised subsequently

(6) If a question as described in subsection (5) arises after a member or panel has been assigned and the requirements of that subsection are not met, the inquiry shall nevertheless proceed with the member or panel as designated.

R.S., 1985, c. H-6, s. 49; R.S., 1985, c. 31 (1st Supp.), s. 66; 1998, c. 9, s. 27

Conduct of inquiry

50 (1) After due notice to the Commission, the complainant, the person against whom the complaint was made and, at the discretion of the member or panel conducting the inquiry, any other interested party, the member or panel shall inquire into the complaint and shall give all parties to whom notice has been given a full and ample opportunity, in person or through counsel, to appear at the inquiry, present evidence and make representations.

Power to determine questions of law or fact

(2) In the course of hearing and determining any matter under inquiry, the member or panel may decide all questions of law or fact necessary to determining the matter.

Additional powers

(3) In relation to a hearing of the inquiry, the member or panel may

(a) in the same manner and to the same extent as a superior court of record, summon and enforce the attendance of witnesses and compel them to give oral or written evidence on oath and to produce any documents and things that the member or panel considers necessary for the full hearing and consideration of the complaint;

(b) administer oaths;

(c) subject to subsections (4) and (5), receive and accept any evidence and other information, whether on oath or by affidavit or otherwise, that the member or panel sees fit, whether or not that evidence or information is or would be admissible in a court of law;

(d) lengthen or shorten any time limit established by the rules of procedure; and

(e) decide any procedural or evidentiary question arising during the hearing.

Limitation in relation to evidence

(4) The member or panel may not admit or accept as evidence anything that would be inadmissible in a court by reason of any privilege under the law of evidence.

Conciliators as witnesses

(5) A conciliator appointed to settle the complaint is not a competent or compellable witness at the hearing.

Witness fees

(6) Any person summoned to attend the hearing is entitled in the discretion of the member or panel to receive the same fees and allowances as those paid to persons summoned to attend before the Federal Court.

R.S., 1985, c. H-6, s. 50; 1998, c. 9, s. 27

Duty of Commission on appearing

51 In appearing at a hearing, presenting evidence and making representations, the Commission shall adopt such position as, in its opinion, is in the public interest having regard to the nature of the complaint.

R.S., 1985, c. H-6, s. 51; 1998, c. 9, s. 27

Hearing in public subject to confidentiality order

52 (1) An inquiry shall be conducted in public, but the member or panel conducting the inquiry may, on application, take any measures and make any order that the member or panel considers necessary to ensure the

confidentiality of the inquiry if the member or panel is satisfied, during the inquiry or as a result of the inquiry being conducted in public, that

(a) there is a real and substantial risk that matters involving public security will be disclosed;

(b) there is a real and substantial risk to the fairness of the inquiry such that the need to prevent disclosure outweighs the societal interest that the inquiry be conducted in public;

(c) there is a real and substantial risk that the disclosure of personal or other matters will cause undue hardship to the persons involved such that the need to prevent disclosure outweighs the societal interest that the inquiry be conducted in public; or

(d) there is a serious possibility that the life, liberty or security of a person will be endangered.

Confidentiality of application

(2) If the member or panel considers it appropriate, the member or panel may take any measures and make any order that the member or panel considers necessary to ensure the confidentiality of a hearing held in respect of an application under subsection (1).

R.S., 1985, c. H-6, s. 52; 1998, c. 9, s. 27

Complaint dismissed

53 (1) At the conclusion of an inquiry, the member or panel conducting the inquiry shall dismiss the complaint if the member or panel finds that the complaint is not substantiated.

Complaint substantiated

(2) If at the conclusion of the inquiry the member or panel finds that the complaint is substantiated, the member or panel may, subject to section 54, make an order against the person found to be engaging or to have engaged in the discriminatory practice and include in the order any of the following terms that the member or panel considers appropriate:

(a) that the person cease the discriminatory practice and take measures, in consultation with the Commission on the general purposes of the measures, to redress the practice or to prevent the same or a similar practice from occurring in future, including

(i) the adoption of a special program, plan or arrangement referred to in subsection 16(1), or

(ii) making an application for approval and implementing a plan under section 17;

(b) that the person make available to the victim of the discriminatory practice, on the first reasonable occasion, the rights, opportunities or privileges that are being or were denied the victim as a result of the practice;

(c) that the person compensate the victim for any or all of the wages that the victim was deprived of and for any expenses incurred by the victim as a result of the discriminatory practice;

(d) that the person compensate the victim for any or all additional costs of obtaining alternative goods, services, facilities or accommodation and for any expenses incurred by the victim as a result of the discriminatory practice; and

(e) that the person compensate the victim, by an amount not exceeding twenty thousand dollars, for any pain and suffering that the victim experienced as a result of the discriminatory practice.

Special compensation

(3) In addition to any order under subsection (2), the member or panel may order the person to pay such compensation not exceeding twenty thousand dollars to the victim as the member or panel may determine if the member or panel finds that the person is engaging or has engaged in the discriminatory practice wilfully or recklessly.

Interest

(4) Subject to the rules made under section 48.9, an order to pay compensation under this section may include an award of interest at a rate and for a period that the member or panel considers appropriate.

R.S., 1985, c. H-6, s. 53; 1998, c. 9, s. 27

Limitation

54 No order that is made under subsection 53(2) may contain a term

(a) requiring the removal of an individual from a position if that individual accepted employment in that position in good faith; or

(b) requiring the expulsion of an occupant from any premises or accommodation, if that occupant obtained those premises or accommodation in good faith.

R.S., 1985, c. H-6, s. 54; 1998, c. 9, s. 28; 2013, c. 37, s. 4

Definitions

54.1 (1) In this section,

designated groups has the meaning assigned in section 3 of the *Employment Equity Act*; and (*groupes désignés*)

employer means a person who or organization that discharges the obligations of an employer under the *Employment Equity Act*. (*employeur*)

Limitation of order re employment equity

(2) Where a Tribunal finds that a complaint against an employer is substantiated, it may not make an order pursuant to subparagraph 53(2)(a)(i) requiring the employer to adopt a special program, plan or arrangement containing

(a) positive policies and practices designed to ensure that members of designated groups achieve increased representation in the employer's workforce; or

(b) goals and timetables for achieving that increased representation.

Interpretation

(3) For greater certainty, subsection (2) shall not be construed as limiting the power of a Tribunal, under paragraph 53(2)(a), to make an order requiring an employer to cease or otherwise correct a discriminatory practice.

1995, c. 44, s. 50

55 and 56 [Repealed, 1998, c. 9, s. 29]

Enforcement of order

57 An order under section 53 may, for the purpose of enforcement, be made an order of the Federal Court by following the usual practice and

procedure or by the Commission filing in the Registry of the Court a copy of the order certified to be a true copy.

R.S., 1985, c. H-6, s. 57; 1998, c. 9, s. 29; 2013, c. 37, s. 5

Application respecting disclosure of information

58 (1) Subject to subsection (2), if an investigator or a member or panel of the Tribunal requires the disclosure of any information and a minister of the Crown or any other interested person objects to its disclosure, the Commission may apply to the Federal Court for a determination of the matter and the Court may take any action that it considers appropriate.

Canada Evidence Act

(2) An objection to disclosure shall be determined in accordance with the *Canada Evidence Act* if

(a) under subsection (1), a minister of the Crown or other official objects to the disclosure in accordance with sections 37 to 37.3 or section 39 of that Act;

(b) within 90 days after the day on which the Commission applies to the Federal Court, a minister of the Crown or other official objects to the disclosure in accordance with sections 37 to 37.3 or section 39 of that Act; or

(c) at any time, an objection to the disclosure is made, or a certificate is issued, in accordance with sections 38 to 38.13 of that Act.

R.S., 1985, c. H-6, s. 58; 1998, c. 9, s. 30; 2001, c. 41, s. 45

Intimidation or discrimination

59 No person shall threaten, intimidate or discriminate against an individual because that individual has made a complaint or given evidence or assisted in any way in respect of the initiation or prosecution of a complaint or other proceeding under this Part, or because that individual proposes to do so.

1976-77, c. 33, s. 45

Offences and Punishment

Offence

60 (1) Every person is guilty of an offence who

(a) [Repealed, 1998, c. 9, s. 31]

(b) obstructs a member or panel in carrying out its functions under this Part; or

(c) contravenes subsection 11(6) or 43(3) or section 59.

Punishment

(2) A person who is guilty of an offence under subsection (1) is liable on summary conviction to a fine not exceeding $50,000.

Prosecution of employer or employee organization

(3) A prosecution for an offence under this section may be brought against an employer organization or employee organization and in the name of the organization and, for the purpose of the prosecution, the organization is deemed to be a person and any act or thing done or omitted by an officer or agent of the organization within the scope of their authority to act on behalf of the organization is deemed to be an act or thing done or omitted by the organization.

Consent of Attorney General

(4) A prosecution for an offence under this section may not be instituted except by or with the consent of the Attorney General of Canada.

Limitation period

(5) A prosecution for an offence under this section may not be instituted more than one year after the subject-matter of the proceedings arose.

R.S., 1985, c. H-6, s. 60; 1998, c. 9, s. 31

Reports

Annual report of Commission

61 (1) The Commission shall, within three months after December 31 in each year, prepare and submit to Parliament a report on the activities of the Commission under this Part and Part II for that year, including references to and comments on any matter referred to in paragraph 27(1)(e) or (g) that it considers appropriate.

Special reports

(2) The Commission may, at any time, prepare and submit to Parliament a special report referring to and commenting on any matter within the scope of its powers, duties and functions if, in its opinion, the matter is of such urgency or importance that a report on it should not be deferred until the time provided for submission of its next annual report under subsection (1).

Annual report of Tribunal

(3) The Tribunal shall, within three months after December 31 in each year, prepare and submit to Parliament a report on its activities under this Act for that year.

Transmission of report

(4) Every report under this section shall be submitted by being transmitted to the Speaker of the Senate and to the Speaker of the House of Commons for tabling in those Houses.

R.S., 1985, c. H-6, s. 61; 1998, c. 9, s. 32

Minister Responsible

Minister of Justice

61.1 The Minister of Justice is responsible for this Act, and the powers of the Governor in Council to make regulations under this Act, with the exception of section 29, are exercisable on the recommendation of that Minister.

1998, c. 9, s. 32

Application

Limitation

62 (1) This Part and Parts I and II do not apply to or in respect of any superannuation or pension fund or plan established by an Act of Parliament enacted before March 1, 1978.

Review of Acts referred to in subsection (1)

(2) The Commission shall keep under review those Acts of Parliament enacted before March 1, 1978 by which any superannuation or pension fund or plan is established and, where the Commission deems it to be

appropriate, it may include in a report mentioned in section 61 reference to and comment on any provision of any of those Acts that in its opinion is inconsistent with the principle described in section 2.

1976-77, c. 33, s. 48

Application in the territories

63 Where a complaint under this Part relates to an act or omission that occurred in Yukon, the Northwest Territories or Nunavut, it may not be dealt with under this Part unless the act or omission could be the subject of a complaint under this Part had it occurred in a province.

R.S., 1985, c. H-6, s. 63; 1993, c. 28, s. 78; 2002, c. 7, s. 127

Canadian Forces and Royal Canadian Mounted Police

64 For the purposes of this Part and Parts I and II, members of the Canadian Forces and the Royal Canadian Mounted Police are deemed to be employed by the Crown.

1976-77, c. 33, s. 48

Acts of employees, etc.

65 (1) Subject to subsection (2), any act or omission committed by an officer, a director, an employee or an agent of any person, association or organization in the course of the employment of the officer, director, employee or agent shall, for the purposes of this Act, be deemed to be an act or omission committed by that person, association or organization.

Exculpation

(2) An act or omission shall not, by virtue of subsection (1), be deemed to be an act or omission committed by a person, association or organization if it is established that the person, association or organization did not consent to the commission of the act or omission and exercised all due diligence to prevent the act or omission from being committed and, subsequently, to mitigate or avoid the effect thereof.

1980-81-82-83, c. 143, s. 23

PART IV

Application

Binding on Her Majesty

66 (1) This Act is binding on Her Majesty in right of Canada, except in matters respecting the Yukon Government or the Government of the Northwest Territories or Nunavut.

(2) [Repealed, 2002, c. 7, s. 128]

(3) [Repealed, 2014, c. 2, s. 11]

Idem

(4) The exception referred to in subsection (1) shall come into operation in respect of the Government of Nunavut on a day to be fixed by order of the Governor in Council.

R.S., 1985, c. H-6, s. 66; 1993, c. 28, s. 78; 2002, c. 7, s. 128; 2014, c. 2, s. 11

67 [Repealed, 2008, c. 30, s. 1]

RELATED PROVISIONS

— R.S., 1985, c. 31 (1st Supp.), s. 68

Transitional

68 Every Tribunal appointed prior to the coming into force of this Act shall continue to act as though this Part had not come into force.

— 1998, c. 9, s. 33

Definition of commencement day

33 (1) In this section, commencement day means the day on which this section comes into force.

Members cease to hold office

(2) Subject to subsections (3), (4) and (5), the members of the Human Rights Tribunal Panel cease to hold office on the commencement day.

Continuing jurisdiction of Human Rights Tribunal

(3) The members of any Human Rights Tribunal appointed under the *Canadian Human Rights Act* before the commencement day have jurisdiction with respect to any inquiry into the complaint in respect of which the Human Rights Tribunal was appointed.

Continuing jurisdiction of Review Tribunal

(4) The members of any Review Tribunal constituted under the *Canadian Human Rights Act* before the commencement day have jurisdiction with respect to any appeal against a decision or order of a Human Rights Tribunal.

Continuing jurisdiction of Employment Equity Review Tribunal

(5) The members of any Employment Equity Review Tribunal established under section 28 or 39 of the *Employment Equity Act* before the commencement day have jurisdiction over any matter in respect of which the Tribunal was established.

Supervision by Chairperson of Canadian Human Rights Tribunal

(6) The Chairperson of the Canadian Human Rights Tribunal has supervision over and direction of the work of any Human Rights Tribunal, Review Tribunal or Employment Equity Review Tribunal referred to in subsection (3), (4) or (5).

Remuneration

(7) Each member of a Human Rights Tribunal, Review Tribunal or Employment Equity Review Tribunal referred to in subsection (3), (4) or (5), other than such a member who is appointed as a full-time member of the Canadian Human Rights Tribunal, shall be paid such remuneration as may be fixed by the Governor in Council.

Travel expenses

(8) Each member of a Human Rights Tribunal, Review Tribunal or Employment Equity Review Tribunal referred to in subsection (3), (4) or (5) is entitled to be paid travel and living expenses incurred in carrying out duties as a member of that Tribunal while absent from their place of residence, but the expenses must not exceed the maximum limits authorized by Treasury Board directive for employees of the Government of Canada.

— 1998, c. 9, s. 34

Commission employees serving the Human Rights Tribunal Panel

34 (1) This Act does not affect the status of an employee who, immediately before the coming into force of this subsection, occupied a position in the Canadian Human Rights Commission and performed services on a full-time basis for the Human Rights Tribunal Panel, except that the employee shall, on the coming into force of this subsection, occupy that position in the Canadian Human Rights Tribunal.

Definition of employee

(2) In this section, employee has the same meaning as in subsection 2(1) of the *Public Service Employment Act.*

— 2008, c. 30, s. 1.1

Aboriginal rights

1.1 For greater certainty, the repeal of section 67 of the *Canadian Human Rights Act* shall not be construed so as to abrogate or derogate from the protection provided for existing aboriginal or treaty rights of the aboriginal peoples of Canada by the recognition and affirmation of those rights in section 35 of the *Constitution Act*, 1982.

— 2008, c. 30, s. 1.2

Regard to legal traditions and customary laws

1.2 In relation to a complaint made under the *Canadian Human Rights Act* against a First Nation government, including a band council, tribal council or governing authority operating or administering programs and services under the *Indian Act*, this Act shall be interpreted and applied in a manner that gives due regard to First Nations legal traditions and customary laws, particularly the balancing of individual rights and interests against collective rights and interests, to the extent that they are consistent with the principle of gender equality.

— 2008, c. 30, s. 2

Comprehensive review

2 (1) Within five years after the day on which this Act receives royal assent, a comprehensive review of the effects of the repeal of section 67 of the *Canadian Human Rights Act* shall be jointly undertaken by the

Government of Canada and any organizations identified by the Minister of Indian Affairs and Northern Development as being, in the aggregate, representative of the interests of First Nations peoples throughout Canada.

Report

(2) A report on the review referred to in subsection (1) shall be submitted to both Houses of Parliament within one year after the day on which the review is undertaken under that subsection.

— 2008, c. 30, s. 3

Grace period

3 Despite section 1, an act or omission by any First Nation government, including a band council, tribal council or governing authority operating or administering programs or services under the *Indian Act*, that was made in the exercise of powers or the performance of duties and functions conferred or imposed by or under that Act shall not constitute the basis for a complaint under Part III of the *Canadian Human Rights Act* if it occurs within 36 months after the day on which this Act receives royal assent.

— 2008, c. 30, s. 4

Study to be undertaken

4 The Government of Canada, together with the appropriate organizations representing the First Nations peoples of Canada, shall, within the period referred to in section 3, undertake a study to identify the extent of the preparation, capacity and fiscal and human resources that will be required in order for First Nations communities and organizations to comply with the *Canadian Human Rights Act*. The Government of Canada shall report to both Houses of Parliament on the findings of that study before the expiration of the period referred to in section 3.

— 2009, c. 2, s. 395

Interpretation

395 Unless the context otherwise requires, words and expressions used in sections 396 and 397 have the same meaning as in the *Public Sector Equitable Compensation Act.*

— 2009, c. 2, s. 396

Complaints before Canadian Human Rights Commission

396 (1) The following complaints with respect to employees that are before the Canadian Human Rights Commission on the day on which this Act receives royal assent, or that are filed with that Commission during the period beginning on that day and ending on the day on which section 399 comes into force, shall, despite section 44 of the *Canadian Human Rights Act*, without delay, be referred by the Commission to the Board:

(a) complaints based on section 7 or 10 of the *Canadian Human Rights Act*, if the complaint is in respect of the employer establishing or maintaining differences in wages between male and female employees; and

(b) complaints based on section 11 of the *Canadian Human Rights Act.*

Application of this section

(2) The complaints referred to in subsection (1) shall be dealt with by the Board as required by this section.

Powers of Board

(3) The Board has, in relation to a complaint referred to it, in addition to the powers conferred on it under the Public Service Labour Relations Act, the power to interpret and apply sections 7, 10 and 11 of the *Canadian Human Rights Act*, and the Equal Wages Guidelines, 1986, in respect of employees, even after the coming into force of section 399.

Summary examination

(4) The Board shall review the complaint in a summary way and shall refer it to the employer that is the subject of the complaint, or to the employer that is the subject of the complaint and the bargaining agent of the employees who filed the complaint, as the Board considers

appropriate, unless it appears to the Board that the complaint is trivial, frivolous or vexatious or was made in bad faith.

Power to assist

(5) If the Board refers a complaint under subsection (4) to an employer, or to an employer and a bargaining agent, it may assist them in resolving any matters relating to the complaint by any means that it considers appropriate.

Hearing

(6) If the employer, or the employer and the bargaining agent, as the case may be, do not resolve the matters relating to the complaint within 180 days after the complaint is referred to them, or any longer period or periods that may be authorized by the Board, the Board shall schedule a hearing.

Procedure

(7) The Board shall determine its own procedure but shall give full opportunity to the employer, or the employer and the bargaining agent, as the case may be, to present evidence and make submissions to it.

Decision

(8) The Board shall make a decision in writing in respect of the complaint and send a copy of its decision with the reasons for it to the employer, or the employer and the bargaining agent, as the case may be.

Restriction

(9) The Board has, in relation to complaints referred to in this section, the power to make any order that a member or panel may make under section 53 of the *Canadian Human Rights Act*, except that no monetary remedy may be granted by the Board in respect of the complaint other than a lump sum payment, and the payment may be only in respect of a period that ends on or before the day on which section 394 comes into force.

— 2009, c. 2, s. 397

Complaints before Canadian Human Rights Tribunal

397 (1) Subject to subsections (2) and (3), the Canadian Human Rights Tribunal shall inquire into the following complaints with respect to employees that are before it on the day on which this Act receives royal assent:

(a) complaints based on section 7 or 10 of the *Canadian Human Rights Act*, if the complaint is in respect of the employer establishing or maintaining differences in wages between male and female employees; and

(b) complaints based on section 11 of the *Canadian Human Rights Act*.

Powers of Tribunal

(2) If section 399 is in force when the Canadian Human Rights Tribunal inquires into a complaint referred to in subsection (1),

(a) complaints referred to in paragraph (1)(a) shall be dealt with as if sections 7 and 10 of the *Canadian Human Rights Act* still applied to those employees; and

(b) complaints referred to in paragraph (1)(b) shall be dealt with as if section 11 of the *Canadian Human Rights Act* and the Equal Wage Guidelines, 1986 still applied to those employees.

Limitation

(3) No monetary remedy may be granted by the Canadian Human Rights Tribunal in respect of a complaint referred to in subsection (1) other than a lump sum payment, and the payment may only be in respect of a period that ends on or before the day on which section 394 comes into force.

— 2012, c. 1, par. 165(a)

Pardons in effect — references in other legislation

165 A reference to a record suspension in the following provisions, as enacted by this Part, is deemed also to be a reference to a pardon that is granted or issued under the *Criminal Records Act*:

(a) the definition conviction for an offence for which a pardon has been granted or in respect of which a record suspension has been ordered in section 25 of the *Canadian Human Rights Act*;

AMENDMENTS NOT IN FORCE

— 2009, c. 2, s. 399

399 The *Canadian Human Rights Act* is amended by adding the following after section 40.1:

Non-application of sections 7, 10 and 11

40.2 The Commission does not have jurisdiction to deal with complaints made against an employer within the meaning of the *Public Sector Equitable Compensation Act* alleging that

(a) the employer has engaged in a discriminatory practice referred to in section 7 or 10, if the complaint is in respect of the employer establishing or maintaining differences in wages between male and female employees; or

(b) the employer has engaged in a discriminatory practice referred to in section 11.

— 2018, c. 27, s. 419

419 Subsections 26(1) and (2) of the *Canadian Human Rights Act* are replaced by the following:

Commission established

26 (1) A commission is established to be known as the Canadian Human Rights Commission, in this Act referred to as the "Commission", consisting of a Chief Commissioner, a Deputy Chief Commissioner, a member referred to as the "Pay Equity Commissioner" and not less than three or more than six other members, to be appointed by the Governor in Council.

Members

(2) The Chief Commissioner, the Deputy Chief Commissioner and the Pay Equity Commissioner are full-time members of the Commission and the other members may be appointed as full-time or part-time members of the Commission.

Required qualifications — Pay Equity Commissioner

(2.1) The Governor in Council must take into consideration, in appointing the Pay Equity Commissioner, knowledge and experience in relation to pay equity matters.

— 2018, c. 27, s. 420

420 The Act is amended by adding the following after section 32:

Pay Equity Unit

32.1 The officers and employees of the Commission that support the Pay Equity Commissioner in the exercise of his or her powers and the performance of his or her duties and functions under the *Pay Equity Act* may be referred to as the "Pay Equity Unit".

— 2018, c. 27, s. 421

421 Subsection 36(1) of the Act is replaced by the following:

Establishment of divisions

36 (1) Subject to section 36.1, for the purposes of the affairs of the Commission, the Chief Commissioner may establish divisions of the Commission and all or any of the powers, duties and functions of the Commission, except the making of by-laws, may, as directed by the Commission, be exercised or performed by all or any of those divisions.

— 2018, c. 27, s. 422

422 The Act is amended by adding the following after section 36:

Pay Equity Division

36.1 (1) On receipt of a complaint under section 40 alleging a discriminatory practice under section 11, the Chief Commissioner must establish, for the purposes of Part III, a Pay Equity Division of the Commission of which the Pay Equity Commissioner is the presiding officer.

Complaints — section 11

(2) A Pay Equity Division established under subsection (1) must exercise the powers and perform the duties and functions of the Commission under Part III with respect to the complaint in question.

— 2018, c. 27, s. 423

423 The Act is amended by adding the following after section 38:

Pay Equity Commissioner

Powers, duties and functions

38.1 In addition to being a member of the Commission, the Pay Equity Commissioner must exercise the powers and perform the duties and functions assigned to him or her by the *Pay Equity Act*.

Absence or incapacity of Pay Equity Commissioner

38.2 (1) In the event of the absence or incapacity of the Pay Equity Commissioner, or if the office of Pay Equity Commissioner is vacant, the Chief Commissioner may authorize any member of the Commission, other than himself or herself, to exercise the powers and perform the duties and functions of the Pay Equity Commissioner, but no member may be so authorized for a term of more than 90 days without the Governor in Council's approval.

Required qualifications — acting Pay Equity Commissioner

(2) The Chief Commissioner must take into consideration, in appointing the acting Pay Equity Commissioner, knowledge and experience in relation to pay equity matters.

— 2018, c. 27, s. 424

424 Section 40 of the Act is amended by adding the following after subsection (4):

Multiple allegations

(4.1) If a complaint alleging a discriminatory practice under section 11 also includes allegations to which section 11 does not apply, the Pay Equity Division may

(a) exercise the powers and perform the duties and functions of the Commission under this Part with respect to the complaint as filed; or

(b) at any stage after the filing of the complaint, sever the complaint and refer to the Commission some or all of the allegations that do not allege a discriminatory practice under section 11.

New complaint

(4.2) If the Pay Equity Division refers allegations severed from a complaint to the Commission under paragraph (4.1)(b), the Commission is deemed to have received a new complaint for the purposes of section 40.

— 2018, c. 27, s. 425

425 (1) The Act is amended by adding the following after section 40.1:

Non-application of sections 7, 10 and 11

40.2 The Commission does not have jurisdiction to deal with complaints made by an employee, as defined in subsection 3(1) of the *Pay Equity Act*, against an employer that is subject to that Act, alleging that

(a) the employer has engaged in a discriminatory practice referred to in section 7 or 10, if the complaint is in respect of the employer establishing or maintaining differences in wages between male and female employees who are performing work of equal value; or

(b) the employer has engaged in a discriminatory practice referred to in section 11.

(2) Section 40.2 of the Act is renumbered as subsection 40.2(1) and is amended by adding the following:

Parliamentary employees

(2) The Commission does not have jurisdiction to deal with complaints made by an employee, within the meaning of section 86.1 of the *Parliamentary Employment and Staff Relations Act*, against an employer, within the meaning of that same section, alleging that the employer has engaged in a discriminatory practice referred to in subsection (1).

— 2018, c. 27, s. 426

426 (1) Subsection 48.1(1) of the Act is replaced by the following:

Establishment of Tribunal

48.1 (1) There is hereby established a tribunal to be known as the Canadian Human Rights Tribunal consisting, subject to subsection (6), of a maximum of 18 members, including a Chairperson and a Vice-chairperson, as may be appointed by the Governor in Council.

(2) Section 48.1 of the Act is amended by adding the following after subsection (4):

Knowledge and experience — pay equity

(4.1) Appointments must be made having regard to the need for adequate knowledge and experience in pay equity matters among the members of the Tribunal.

— 2018, c. 27, s. 428

Complaints — *Canadian Human Rights Act*

428 The *Canadian Human Rights Act*, as it read immediately before the day on which this section comes into force, applies with respect to any complaint filed before that day under section 40 of that Act, other than a complaint referred to in subsection 396(1) of the *Budget Implementation Act, 2009*, as amended by subsection 431(1) of this Act.

— 2018, c. 27, s. 430

430 Section 395 of the Act is repealed.

— 2018, c. 27, s. 431

431 (1) The portion of subsection 396(1) of the Act before paragraph (a) is replaced by the following:

Complaints before Canadian Human Rights Commission

396 (1) The following complaints with respect to employees that are before the Canadian Human Rights Commission on the day on which this Act receives royal assent, or that are filed with that Commission during the period beginning on that day and ending on the day on which subsection 425(1) of the Budget Implementation Act, 2018, No. 2 comes into force, shall, despite section 44 of the *Canadian Human Rights Act*, without delay, be referred by the Commission to the Board:

(2) Subsection 396(3) of the Act is replaced by the following:

Powers of Board

(3) The Board has, in relation to a complaint referred to it, in addition to the powers conferred on it under the *Federal Public Sector Labour Relations Act*, the power to interpret and apply sections 7, 10 and 11 of the *Canadian Human Rights Act*, and the Equal Wages Guidelines, 1986, in respect of employees, even after the coming into force of subsection 425(1) of the Budget Implementation Act 2018, No. 2.

(3) Subsection 396(9) of the Act is replaced by the following:

Restriction

(9) The Board has, in relation to complaints referred to in this section, the power to make any order that a member or panel may make under section 53 of the *Canadian Human Rights Act*, except that no monetary remedy may be granted by the Board in respect of the complaint other than a lump sum payment, and the payment may be only in respect of a period that ends on or before the day on which subsection 425(1) of the Budget Implementation Act, 2018, No. 2 comes into force.

(4) Section 396 of the Act is repealed.

— 2018, c. 27, s. 432

432 Sections 397 to 399 of the Act are repealed.

— 2018, c. 27, s. 439

Bill C-81

439 (1) Subsections (2) to (4) apply if Bill C-81, introduced in the 1st session of the 42nd Parliament and entitled the *Accessible Canada Act* (in this section referred to as the "other Act"), receives royal assent.

(2) On the first day on which both section 148 of the other Act and section 419 of this Act are in force, subsections 26(1) and (2) of the *Canadian Human Rights Act* are replaced by the following:

Commission established

26 (1) A commission is established to be known as the Canadian Human Rights Commission, in this Act referred to as the "Commission", consisting of a Chief Commissioner, a Deputy Chief Commissioner, members referred to as the "Accessibility Commissioner" and the "Pay Equity Commissioner" and not less than three or more than six other members, to be appointed by the Governor in Council.

Members

(2) The Chief Commissioner, the Deputy Chief Commissioner, the Accessibility Commissioner and the Pay Equity Commissioner are full-time members of the Commission and the other members may be appointed as full-time or part-time members of the Commission.

(3) On the first day on which both section 151 of the other Act and section 420 of this Act are in force, section 32.1 of the *Canadian Human Rights Act*, as enacted by section 420 of this Act, is renumbered as section 32.2 and is repositioned accordingly if required.

(4) On the first day on which both section 152 of the other Act and section 423 of this Act are in force, sections 38.1 and 38.2 of the *Canadian Human Rights Act*, as enacted by section 423 of this Act, are renumbered as sections 38.3 and 38.4, respectively, and those sections — and the heading before that section 38.1, as enacted by section 423 of this Act — are repositioned accordingly if required.

III. Canadian Charter of Rights and Freedoms

CONSTITUTION ACT, 1982

PART I

Canadian Charter of Rights and Freedoms[186]

Whereas Canada is founded upon principles that recognize the supremacy of God and the rule of law:

Guarantee of Rights and Freedoms

Rights and freedoms in Canada

1. The *Canadian Charter of Rights and Freedoms* guarantees the rights and freedoms set out in it subject only to such reasonable limits prescribed by law as can be demonstrably justified in a free and democratic society.

Fundamental Freedoms

Fundamental freedoms

2. Everyone has the following fundamental freedoms:

(*a*) freedom of conscience and religion;

(*b*) freedom of thought, belief, opinion and expression, including freedom of the press and other media of communication;

(*c*) freedom of peaceful assembly; and

(*d*) freedom of association.

---

[186] "Constitution Act, 1982", Government of Canada, last updated October 29, 2020, https://laws-lois.justice.gc.ca/eng/const/page-15.html

Democratic Rights

Democratic rights of citizens

3. Every citizen of Canada has the right to vote in an election of members of the House of Commons or of a legislative assembly and to be qualified for membership therein.

Maximum duration of legislative bodies

4. (1) No House of Commons and no legislative assembly shall continue for longer than five years from the date fixed for the return of the writs at a general election of its members.

Continuation in special circumstances

(2) In time of real or apprehended war, invasion or insurrection, a House of Commons may be continued by Parliament and a legislative assembly may be continued by the legislature beyond five years if such continuation is not opposed by the votes of more than one-third of the members of the House of Commons or the legislative assembly, as the case may be.

Annual sitting of legislative bodies

5. There shall be a sitting of Parliament and of each legislature at least once every twelve months.

Mobility Rights

Mobility of citizens

6. (1) Every citizen of Canada has the right to enter, remain in and leave Canada.

Rights to move and gain livelihood

(2) Every citizen of Canada and every person who has the status of a permanent resident of Canada has the right

(*a*) to move to and take up residence in any province; and

(*b*) to pursue the gaining of a livelihood in any province.

Limitation

(3) The rights specified in subsection (2) are subject to

(*a*) any laws or practices of general application in force in a province other than those that discriminate among persons primarily on the basis of province of present or previous residence; and

(*b*) any laws providing for reasonable residency requirements as a qualification for the receipt of publicly provided social services.

Affirmative action programs

(4) Subsections (2) and (3) do not preclude any law, program or activity that has as its object the amelioration in a province of conditions of individuals in that province who are socially or economically disadvantaged if the rate of employment in that province is below the rate of employment in Canada.

Legal Rights

Life, liberty and security of person

7. Everyone has the right to life, liberty and security of the person and the right not to be deprived thereof except in accordance with the principles of fundamental justice.

Search or seizure

8. Everyone has the right to be secure against unreasonable search or seizure.

Detention or imprisonment

9. Everyone has the right not to be arbitrarily detained or imprisoned.

Arrest or detention

10. Everyone has the right on arrest or detention

(*a*) to be informed promptly of the reasons therefor;

(*b*) to retain and instruct counsel without delay and to be informed of that right; and

(*c*) to have the validity of the detention determined by way of *habeas corpus* and to be released if the detention is not lawful.

Proceedings in criminal and penal matters

11. Any person charged with an offence has the right

(*a*) to be informed without unreasonable delay of the specific offence;

(*b*) to be tried within a reasonable time;

(*c*) not to be compelled to be a witness in proceedings against that person in respect of the offence;

(*d*) to be presumed innocent until proven guilty according to law in a fair and public hearing by an independent and impartial tribunal;

(*e*) not to be denied reasonable bail without just cause;

(*f*) except in the case of an offence under military law tried before a military tribunal, to the benefit of trial by jury where the maximum punishment for the offence is imprisonment for five years or a more severe punishment;

(*g*) not to be found guilty on account of any act or omission unless, at the time of the act or omission, it constituted an offence under Canadian or international law or was criminal according to the general principles of law recognized by the community of nations;

(*h*) if finally acquitted of the offence, not to be tried for it again and, if finally found guilty and punished for the offence, not to be tried or punished for it again; and

(*i*) if found guilty of the offence and if the punishment for the offence has been varied between the time of commission and the time of sentencing, to the benefit of the lesser punishment.

Treatment or punishment

12. Everyone has the right not to be subjected to any cruel and unusual treatment or punishment.

Self-crimination

13. A witness who testifies in any proceedings has the right not to have any incriminating evidence so given used to incriminate that witness in any other proceedings, except in a prosecution for perjury or for the giving of contradictory evidence.

Interpreter

14. A party or witness in any proceedings who does not understand or speak the language in which the proceedings are conducted or who is deaf has the right to the assistance of an interpreter.

Equality Rights

Equality before and under law and equal protection and benefit of law

15. (1) Every individual is equal before and under the law and has the right to the equal protection and equal benefit of the law without discrimination and, in particular, without discrimination based on race, national or ethnic origin, colour, religion, sex, age or mental or physical disability.

Affirmative action programs

(2) Subsection (1) does not preclude any law, program or activity that has as its object the amelioration of conditions of disadvantaged individuals or groups including those that are disadvantaged because of race, national or ethnic origin, colour, religion, sex, age or mental or physical disability.

Official Languages of Canada

Official languages of Canada

16. (1) English and French are the official languages of Canada and have equality of status and equal rights and privileges as to their use in all institutions of the Parliament and government of Canada.

Official languages of New Brunswick

(2) English and French are the official languages of New Brunswick and have equality of status and equal rights and privileges as to their use in all institutions of the legislature and government of New Brunswick.

Advancement of status and use

(3) Nothing in this Charter limits the authority of Parliament or a legislature to advance the equality of status or use of English and French.

English and French linguistic communities in New Brunswick

16.1 (1) The English linguistic community and the French linguistic community in New Brunswick have equality of status and equal rights and privileges, including the right to distinct educational institutions and such distinct cultural institutions as are necessary for the preservation and promotion of those communities.

Role of the legislature and government of New Brunswick

(2) The role of the legislature and government of New Brunswick to preserve and promote the status, rights and privileges referred to in subsection (1) is affirmed.

Proceedings of Parliament

17. (1) Everyone has the right to use English or French in any debates and other proceedings of Parliament.

Proceedings of New Brunswick legislature

(2) Everyone has the right to use English or French in any debates and other proceedings of the legislature of New Brunswick.

Parliamentary statutes and records

18. (1) The statutes, records and journals of Parliament shall be printed and published in English and French and both language versions are equally authoritative.

New Brunswick statutes and records

(2) The statutes, records and journals of the legislature of New Brunswick shall be printed and published in English and French and both language versions are equally authoritative.

Proceedings in courts established by Parliament

19. (1) Either English or French may be used by any person in, or in any pleading in or process issuing from, any court established by Parliament.

Proceedings in New Brunswick courts

(2) Either English or French may be used by any person in, or in any pleading in or process issuing from, any court of New Brunswick.

Communications by public with federal institutions

20. (1) Any member of the public in Canada has the right to communicate with, and to receive available services from, any head or central office of an institution of the Parliament or government of Canada in English or French, and has the same right with respect to any other office of any such institution where

(*a*) there is a significant demand for communications with and services from that office in such language; or (*b*) due to the nature of the office, it is reasonable that communications with and services from that office be available in both English and French.

Communications by public with New Brunswick institutions

(2) Any member of the public in New Brunswick has the right to communicate with, and to receive available services from, any office of an institution of the legislature or government of New Brunswick in English or French.

Continuation of existing constitutional provisions

21. Nothing in sections 16 to 20 abrogates or derogates from any right, privilege or obligation with respect to the English and French languages, or either of them, that exists or is continued by virtue of any other provision of the Constitution of Canada.

Rights and privileges preserved

22. Nothing in sections 16 to 20 abrogates or derogates from any legal or customary right or privilege acquired or enjoyed either before or after the coming into force of this Charter with respect to any language that is not English or French.

Minority Language Educational Rights

Language of instruction

23. (1) Citizens of Canada

(*a*) whose first language learned and still understood is that of the English or French linguistic minority population of the province in which they reside, or

(*b*) who have received their primary school instruction in Canada in English or French and reside in a province where the language in which they received that instruction is the language of the English or French linguistic minority population of the province,

have the right to have their children receive primary and secondary school instruction in that language in that province.

Continuity of language instruction

(2) Citizens of Canada of whom any child has received or is receiving primary or secondary school instruction in English or French in Canada, have the right to have all their children receive primary and secondary school instruction in the same language.

Application where numbers warrant

(3) The right of citizens of Canada under subsections (1) and (2) to have their children receive primary and secondary school instruction in the language of the English or French linguistic minority population of a province

(*a*) applies wherever in the province the number of children of citizens who have such a right is sufficient to warrant the provision to them out of public funds of minority language instruction; and

(*b*) includes, where the number of those children so warrants, the right to have them receive that instruction in minority language educational facilities provided out of public funds.

Enforcement

Enforcement of guaranteed rights and freedoms

24. (1) Anyone whose rights or freedoms, as guaranteed by this Charter, have been infringed or denied may apply to a court of competent jurisdiction to obtain such remedy as the court considers appropriate and just in the circumstances.

Exclusion of evidence bringing administration of justice into disrepute

(2) Where, in proceedings under subsection (1), a court concludes that evidence was obtained in a manner that infringed or denied any rights or freedoms guaranteed by this Charter, the evidence shall be excluded if it is established that, having regard to all the circumstances, the admission of it in the proceedings would bring the administration of justice into disrepute.

General

Aboriginal rights and freedoms not affected by Charter

25. The guarantee in this Charter of certain rights and freedoms shall not be construed so as to abrogate or derogate from any aboriginal, treaty or

other rights or freedoms that pertain to the aboriginal peoples of Canada including

(*a*) any rights or freedoms that have been recognized by the Royal Proclamation of October 7, 1763; and

(*b*) any rights or freedoms that now exist by way of land claims agreements or may be so acquired.

Other rights and freedoms not affected by Charter

26. The guarantee in this Charter of certain rights and freedoms shall not be construed as denying the existence of any other rights or freedoms that exist in Canada.

Multicultural heritage

27. This Charter shall be interpreted in a manner consistent with the preservation and enhancement of the multicultural heritage of Canadians.

Rights guaranteed equally to both sexes

28. Notwithstanding anything in this Charter, the rights and freedoms referred to in it are guaranteed equally to male and female persons.

Rights respecting certain schools preserved

29. Nothing in this Charter abrogates or derogates from any rights or privileges guaranteed by or under the Constitution of Canada in respect of denominational, separate or dissentient schools.

Application to territories and territorial authorities

30. A reference in this Charter to a province or to the legislative assembly or legislature of a province shall be deemed to include a reference to the Yukon Territory and the Northwest Territories, or to the appropriate legislative authority thereof, as the case may be.

Legislative powers not extended

31. Nothing in this Charter extends the legislative powers of any body or authority.

Application of Charter

Application of Charter

32. (1) This Charter applies

(*a*) to the Parliament and government of Canada in respect of all matters within the authority of Parliament including all matters relating to the Yukon Territory and Northwest Territories; and

(*b*) to the legislature and government of each province in respect of all matters within the authority of the legislature of each province.

Exception

(2) Notwithstanding subsection (1), section 15 shall not have effect until three years after this section comes into force.

Exception where express declaration

33. (1) Parliament or the legislature of a province may expressly declare in an Act of Parliament or of the legislature, as the case may be, that the Act or a provision thereof shall operate notwithstanding a provision included in section 2 or sections 7 to 15 of this Charter.

Operation of exception

(2) An Act or a provision of an Act in respect of which a declaration made under this section is in effect shall have such operation as it would have but for the provision of this Charter referred to in the declaration.

Five year limitation

(3) A declaration made under subsection (1) shall cease to have effect five years after it comes into force or on such earlier date as may be specified in the declaration.

Re-enactment

(4) Parliament or the legislature of a province may re-enact a declaration made under subsection (1).

Five year limitation

(5) Subsection (3) applies in respect of a re-enactment made under subsection (4).

Citation

Citation

34. This Part may be cited as the *Canadian Charter of Rights and Freedoms*.

~ The End ~

www.ingramcontent.com/pod-product-compliance
Lightning Source LLC
LaVergne TN
LVHW010838120826
845149LV00017B/3152

* 9 7 8 0 9 8 8 1 2 1 7 0 6 *